Kerrin-Sina Arfsten

The Minuteman Civil Defense Corps

Hamburger Studien zur Kriminologie und Kriminalpolitik

Herausgegeben von

Prof. Dr. Susanne Krasmann
Prof. Dr. Fritz Sack
Prof. Dr. Sebastian Scheerer
Prof. Dr. Klaus Sessar
Prof. Dr. Bernhard Villmow
Prof. Dr. Peter Wetzels

Band 48

LIT

Kerrin-Sina Arfsten

The Minuteman Civil Defense Corps

Border Vigilantism, Immigration Control and Security on the US-Mexican Border

LIT

Bibliographic information published by the Deutsche Nationalbibliothek
The Deutsche Nationalbibliothek lists this publication in the Deutsche
Nationalbibliografie; detailed bibliographic data are available in the Internet at
http://dnb.d-nb.de.

ISBN 978-3-643-10703-9

A catalogue record for this book is available from the British Library

©LIT VERLAG Dr. W. Hopf Berlin 2010
Fresnostr. 2   D-48159 Münster
Tel. +49 (0) 2 51-620 320   Fax +49 (0) 2 51-922 60 99
e-Mail: lit@lit-verlag.de   http://www.lit-verlag.de

Distribution:
In Germany: LIT Verlag Fresnostr. 2, D-48159 Münster
Tel. +49 (0) 2 51-620 32 22, Fax +49 (0) 2 51-922 60 99, e-Mail: vertrieb@lit-verlag.de

In Austria: Medienlogistik Pichler-ÖBZ, e-mail: mlo@medien-logistik.at

In Switzerland: B + M Buch- und Medienvertrieb, e-mail: order@buch-medien.ch

In the UK: Global Book Marketing, e-mail: mo@centralbooks.com

In North America by:

Transaction Publishers
New Brunswick (U.S.A.) and London (U.K.)

Transaction Publishers
Rutgers University
35 Berrue Circle
Piscataway, NJ 08854

Phone: +1 (732) 445 - 2280
Fax: + 1 (732) 445 - 3138
for orders (U. S. only):
toll free (888) 999 - 6778
e-mail: orders@transactionpub.com

Acknowledgements

This little book has its origins in a Master's thesis that was completed in October 2008 in partial fulfillment of the requirements for the degree of Master of Arts in International Criminology at the *Institut für Kriminologische Sozialforschung*, Hamburg University.

This thesis was greatly improved by my good fortune to discuss ideas with and be inspired by my two advisors at the Institute for Criminological Research, Prof. Dr. Susanne Krasmann and Dr. Bettina Paul. I would also like to thank Prof. Dr. Sebastian Scheerer for his helpful comments and suggestions at the very beginning of this project. All three, I would like to thank for their encouragement and guidance throughout my studies at the Institute and for suggesting that I publish my research in the series *Hamburger Studien zur Kriminologie und Kriminalpolitik*.

As always and most profoundly, I thank my family for providing me with the opportunity to pursue this course of study and for their unconditional love, support and encouragement throughout the years. They have been a tremendous source of inspiration and intellectual stimulation. This book is dedicated to them.

Kerrin-Sina Arfsten

Hamburg, April 2010

TABLE OF CONTENTS

ACKNOWLEDGEMENTS 5
TABLE OF CONTENTS 6
TABLES AND FIGURES 8

PART I: INTRODUCTION AND METHODOLOGY 9
1. INTRODUCTION 10
   1.1 STATE OF THE FIELD 12
   1.2 RESEARCH QUESTION AND OUTLINE OF ARGUMENTATION 13
2. METHODOLOGY 15

PART II: THEORETICAL BACKGROUND 18
3. VIGILANTISM 19
   3.1 JOHNSTON'S CRIMINOLOGICAL DEFINITION 20
   3.2 DELINEATIONS 21
4. THE EMERGENCE OF VIGILANTISM 23
5. IMMIGRATION CONTROL AND SECURITY 25
   5.1 DEFINING "SECURITIZATION" 26
   5.2 "SECURITIZATION" AND IMMIGRATION 27
6. THE HISTORICAL AND LEGAL CONTEXT OF AMERICAN VIGILANTISM 29
   6.1 VIGILANTISM IN UNITED STATES HISTORY 29
   6.2 VIGILANTISM AND THE LAW 32
      6.2.1 Popular Sovereignty 33
      6.2.2 Self-Preservation and the Right to Bear Arms 34
      6.2.3 Citizens' Arrest Statutes 35
      6.2.4 The Invasion-Clause 37
   6.3 THE SIGNIFICANCE OF THE U.S. – MEXICAN BORDER 40
7. BORDER VIGILANTISM 43

PART III: ON THE EMERGENCE OF THE MCDC 45
8. DEFINING THE MINUTEMAN CIVIL DEFENSE CORPS 47

8.1 MOTIVATION 48
8.2 ACTIVITIES 49
8.3 ORGANIZATION 50
8.4 THE MCDC AS BORDER VIGILANTES 51
    8.4.1 Voluntary Activity Engaged in by Autonomous Citizens *52*
    8.4.2 Premeditated Acts of Force or Threatened Force *53*
    8.4.3 Focus on Crime and/or Social Control *55*
    8.4.4 Aim to Offer Security "Guarantees" *56*

9. IMMIGRATION CONTROL AND THE RISE OF THE "CRIMINAL ALIEN" 59

9.1 1875-1940: CREATION OF THE "ILLEGAL IMMIGRANT" 59
9.2 1940-1980: RISE OF THE "CRIMINAL ALIEN" 63
    9.2.1 The Bracero-Program *63*
    9.2.2 Operation Wetback *64*
9.3 1980-2000: "ALIEN INVASION" 67
    9.3.1 Operation Gatekeeper *69*

10. THE MCDC, ILLEGAL IMMIGRATION AND NATIONAL SECURITY 76

11. EXCEPTIONALITY AND THE BORDER 83

12. GLOBALIZATION, PRIVATE SECURITY AND THE ROLE OF THE STATE 86

12.1 GLOBALIZATION AND BORDER CONTROL 86
12.2 GLOBALIZATION AND SECURITY 87
    12.2.1 Risk Society *88*
    12.2.2 The MCDC and Responsibilization *90*

PART III: SUMMARY AND CONCLUSION 92

13. SUMMARY 93

14. CONCLUSION 96

BIBLIOGRAPHY 100

APPENDICES 115

APPENDIX 1: OVERVIEW OF MAJOR U.S. IMMIGRATION LEGISLATION 115
APPENDIX 2: OVERVIEW IMMIGRATION LEGISLATION AFTER SEPTEMBER 11, 2001 123

TABLES AND FIGURES

TABLE 1 JOHNSTON'S SIX KEY FEATURES OF VIGILANTISM 21

FIGURE 1 STRUCTURE OF RELATIONS BETWEEN "GOOD" CITIZENS, CRIMINALS AND THE STATE 24

PART I: INTRODUCTION AND METHODOLOGY

1. Introduction

In March 2005, United States President George Bush was meeting with Mexico's President Vicente Fox when a reporter asked his opinion about "those people who are hunting migrant people along the border"[1]. The President's reply was brief. "I'm against vigilantes in the United States of America," he said, "I'm for enforcing law in a rational way. That's why you got a Border Patrol, and they ought to be in charge of enforcing the border."[2]

Only about a month after President Bush made this statement, the Minuteman Civil Defense Corps (MCDC)[3] launched its first big operation along the U.S. – Mexico border. On April 1, 2005, hundreds of national and international media outlets stood by as citizen border watchers converged on southern Arizona to begin a month-long stakeout for illegal immigrants. For the Minutemen this "spectacle" served one purpose only: to bring national awareness to the "decades-long careless disregard of effective U.S. immigration law enforcement" and to the fact that "America's borders are an ongoing invitation for enemies to destroy us" either by allowing terrorists to slip into the country unnoticed or by "admitting an uncontrolled invasion of millions of people who hold no allegiance whatsoever to the United States" (Gilchrist & Corsi 2006: 7). They felt that the federal government was unwilling or at least unable to secure the borders effectively, and they hoped that by taking the law into their own hands they would "shame the government into doing its job" of controlling the nation's border with Mexico (Baum 2006). While the project was initially met with skepticism and concern by the U.S. Border Patrol and public officials, who feared the possibility of violent confrontations between volunteers and immigrants, after thirty days the border watch ended without any major incidences.

Three years later, I get to experience for myself what this civilian border patrol group is all about. As I drive down Route 286 on our way to

---

[1] http://www.whitehouse.gov/news/releases/2005/03/20050323-5.html; last visited on 11 September 2008.

[2] Ibid.

[3] For the remainder of this book, unless otherwise indicated, any information pertaining to the MCDC organization stems either from the interviews conducted by the author or from the official website of the MCDC, which is available at: www.minutemanhq.com.

the Minuteman Civil Defense Corps' June muster at King's Anvil Ranch, Arizona, I am struck by the beauty of the vast desert valleys and rugged mountains. As far as my eyes can see, clear blue skies stretch out to a seemingly endless horizon. The Arizona desert is not only marked by a unique natural beauty and character, it is also home to an incredible variety of wildlife. From mountain lions, bobcats, coyotes, or *javelinas* to a wide variety of hummingbirds, and more than 13 different kinds of rattlesnakes, everything can be observed here. At the same time, it is easy to see how this serene, wide space can also give rise to feelings of loneliness or isolation when one is not used to it. In the borderlands between Tucson, AZ, and the Mexican border, the ranches are often miles apart. As we pull into King's Anvil Ranch at mile marker 38, the sun is already setting. At dusk, the sun paints the sky in a bright yellow, purple and red against which the *Saguaro*, dark and magnificent, stand tall as Arizona's state flower. Looking out over the desert, my mind almost immediately conjures up romanticized images of the old Wild West.

The moment I actually pull into camp, these images vanish quickly. As I step out of the car, I am greeted by Minuteman volunteers equipped with military fatigues, binoculars and walkie-talkies. All of them carry guns. They are getting ready to go "out on the line," as they say, and have just been paired up into teams and assigned sectors to patrol. Once they are out there, they will stay for at least eight hours, sitting in the dark desert with night-vision devices, waiting for immigrants to come up through the alleys so they can report them to the U.S. Border Patrol. Night missions are considered the most dangerous because of the possibility of drugs being pushed across the border into the United States.

The U.S. – Mexico border is said to be a dangerous place and home to criminal operators of every stripe – smugglers, drug lords and corrupt cops. The U.S. – Mexico border also has the highest number of both legal and illegal crossings of any border in the world. It is guarded, on the United States' side, by more than 10,000 Border Patrol agents - about 9,000 agents more than are currently working along the 4,000-mile U.S. – Canada border. Border Patrol agents are encountered at almost every corner in the small border towns: at convenience stores or gas stations alongside the road or at vehicle checkpoints thirty miles from the actual border. Their presence is clearly felt. Yet, the Minutemen feel that the U.S. Border Patrol needs their assistance in the "monumental task of turning back the tidal wave of people entering our country illegally" (MCDC 2008).

While civilian border patrols are not a new phenomenon along the U.S. – Mexico border, the Minuteman Civil Defense Corps has become much larger and far more influential than any other such group in recent history. With their actions the Minutemen have effectively politicized the issue of homeland security and immigration law and policy in an attempt to persuade the federal government to adopt certain measures, such as, for example, building a fence along the Mexican border. According to Scott Campbell, an organizer with the *San Francisco Bay Area Coalition to Fight the Minutemen*, the group's ideology has even infiltrated the political arena to such extent that, in Arizona alone, at least eighteen anti-immigrant bills have been introduced to the state legislature since the Minutemen's presence was first established (quoted in Romero 2008). That they have gained a significant degree of broader legitimacy is also evidenced by the university speaking tours of co-founder Chris Simcox and his testimonies before government bodies (Doty 2007). Moreover, building on his experience with the Minuteman Civil Defense Corps, "a leading organization for increased border security and illegal immigration reform" (Simcox 2009), Simcox is now running for the U.S. Senate in 2010.

1.1 State of the Field

Despite their apparent influence and a tremendous amount of national and international media attention, only very few researchers have attempted to explain the emergence of the Minuteman phenomenon thus far (see Walker 2007; Doty 2007; Chavez 2008).

Leo Chavez (2008) attributes the emergence of the Minutemen largely to the decades-long public discourse in the United States that has constructed and represented the U.S. - Mexico Border as a place of danger and threat to American society and culture. In view of this, Chavez sees the Minutemen's enlistment of citizens to patrol the border as a "logical consequence" (2008: 34). Whereas this approach is certainly very useful for understanding the historical and cultural context of these civilian patrol groups as well as the powerfulness of public rhetoric, it does not explain why the Minutemen in particular have become so influential, and why they have even gained a certain degree of legitimacy at this very moment in time.

Roxanne Doty (2007) similarly attributes the proliferation of civilian patrol groups to an increased media attention to undocumented immigration since the 1970s. In addition, Doty introduces the Copenhagen School's concept of "securitization" and discusses the role which the securitization of immigration has played in legitimizing the Minutemen. She suggests that as a result of the events of September 11, 2001, and the fears and uncertainty which the attacks caused, the Minutemen were able to link their anti-immigrant agenda to national security. This in turn provided them with the legitimacy they needed to become influential. Christopher Walker (2007) follows the same line of argument. Although providing an insightful discussion of the conceptual and theoretical issues raised by the existence and practice of the Minutemen, Doty's analysis remains just that: a conceptual rather than an empirical analysis. Walker's analysis limits itself to being a purely legal one, looking at immigration legislation in the United States and the vigilante's legal rights.

Lastly, another aspect which might help to explain the rise of civilian border patrol groups is addressed by David Pratten and Atreyee Sen. Pratten and Sen (2008) connect the (re-) emergence of vigilantism to globalization and its associated forces of political and economic liberalization. They suggest that in terms of policing we have entered a new era characterized by a transformation in the governance of security based on economic principles (see also Crawford 1997; Bislev 2004; Crawford et al. 2005; Wood & Dupont 2006). Whereas the state has traditionally been seen as the sole provider of law and order for its citizens, they argue, these traditional distinctions between private and public, centralized and decentralized increasingly become blurred. Politics are increasingly deregulated, sovereignty is franchised and citizens are even encouraged to "engage in a variety of productive security activities" (Johnston 2001: 965). This, Pratten and Sen conclude, creates unparalleled opportunities and motives for citizens to take the law into their own hands.

1.2 Research Question and Outline of Argumentation

This research explores the emergence of the Minuteman Civil Defense Corps as a form of vigilantism at the U.S. - Mexico border. In doing so, it seeks to answer two questions: firstly, why has the Minuteman Civil Defense Corps emerged; and secondly, why has it emerged at this particular moment in time and been able to become as influential as it arguably has.

Sociologist and criminologist Les Johnston's work on vigilantism provides the theoretical framework for answering these two questions. According to Johnston (1996), vigilantism arises from a popular desire of citizens to "do something" when the established order is perceived as threatened and the government fails to satisfactorily control those who pose the threat. In alignment with this two-part definition, this research shows that the Minutemen perceive undocumented immigration as a national security threat and the government as failing to satisfactorily control this threat.

Chavez's and Doty's arguments are then drawn upon to show why the Minutemen perceive undocumented immigration as a national security threat. Pratten and Sen's arguments provide useful insights as to why the Minutemen perceive the government as inefficiently controlling this threat.

Here, it appears that the Minutemen perceive undocumented immigration as a national security threat because (a) immigration policies and official discourses have established the U.S. – Mexico border as a place of danger and threat; and (b) immigration policies and official discourses have constructed the Mexican immigrant as an "illegal alien" and thereby as a source of threat. The research also shows that the Minutemen perceive the government as inefficient when it comes to controlling (illegal) immigration, because globalization (c) has created a conflict between economic (open order) and enforcement (closed border) interests of the United States which has given rise to volatile policymaking, and (d) has led to a privatization and commodification of security that devolves responsibility for security unto the individual rather than the state alone.

Finally, drawing again on Johnston's definition of vigilantism, it is argued that the emergence of the Minuteman Civil Defense Corps must be understood in the context of both the securitization of immigration and the recent transformation in the governance of security.

2. Methodology

Due to the explorative nature of this research, qualitative research methods were used. The required data was gathered from semi-structured, topical interviews and from publically available text material.

For the empirical part of this research, personal interviews were conducted with three leading members of the MCDC who possess special knowledge about the organization. Interviewees included the Vice-President, the State Director of Arizona, and the Chapter Director of Phoenix, AZ. These three interviews offered a good starting point for understanding the emergence of the MCDC because all three interviewees have been with the organization either from its very beginning or from relatively early on.

The interviews were semi-structured in the sense that they were shaped by a set of topics and open-ended questions designed to elicit as much information as possible from the interviewees. I was interested in the interviewees' understanding, knowledge and insights regarding the circumstances which led to the founding of the MCDC, the organization's goals and its perceived success. Most topics and questions were not presented in a precise order or with identical wording but rather matched the flow and choice of topics offered by the interviewees. The length of the interviews ranged from 1 ¼ to 2 ½ hours.

For the theoretical and conceptual part, literature was reviewed. Aside from scholarly publications on vigilantism and security, this research looked at legal documentation, such as immigration laws or the Arizona Statutes. Additionally, a vast amount of literature from various disciplines exists on migration to and from the United States in general (see e.g. Espenshade 1995; Durand & Massey & Parrado 1999; Hanson & Spilimbergo 1999), on U.S. immigration control policy, its history and its effects (see e.g. Tichenor 1994; Cornelius 2001; Rudolph 2003) and the history of the U.S. – Mexico border (see Jamail 1981; Bustamante 1992; Alvarez 1995; Bersin 1996). This was drawn on to provide the historical, cultural and legislative context for this research.

Furthermore, this research made use of the wide variety of media products (newspaper articles, journals, documentaries, internet websites etc.) which are available on the MCDC specifically and other border vigilante groups more generally. The MCDC's website itself, of course, provided a rich ground for information (see MCDC 2008).

The state of Arizona was chosen because, on the one hand, the MCDC originated and is headquartered in this state and, on the other hand, it is said to be a precursor for immigration legislation in the United States (Doty 2007). Arizona is also one of the five states with the largest population of foreign-born from Mexico and, since the tightening of border controls in other states, is said to have become the "new illegal gateway" to America (see Ellingwood 2004; Hayworth 2006; Moser 2006).

After the data was collected, the interviews were analyzed using a form of content analysis. First, the interviews were transcribed and reviewed carefully with regard to identifying concepts and themes. Following this preliminary analysis, the transcribed interviews were reviewed again and coded for the themes and concepts identified previously. All the material from the interviews that spoke to one theme or concept was then pulled out and put into one category. Finally, the data was compared within categories to look for variations and nuances in meaning, and across categories in the hopes of discovering connections between themes.

Last but not least, a word on what is meant by the term "illegal immigrant" in this work. In migration literature it is generally differentiated between several distinct categories of migrants, such as *legal-legal*, *illegal-legal* or *illegal-illegal* (see e.g. Beare 1999). These distinctions are based on the mode in which a migrant arrives in a foreign country. For example, someone who enters the country legally with a time-specific visa and then fails to return to his or her country of origin is considered to fall under the category *legal-illegal*. This work does not differentiate between these categories.

In this work, the term "legal immigrant" is generally understood to be a person of non-U.S. origin who migrates to the United States and is admitted to the United States as a lawful permanent resident. The word "alien" is used in the same sense as it is typically used by the U.S. government: to describe a foreign-born person who is not a citizen by naturalization or parentage. The term "illegal immigrant" is used interchangeably with the terms "unauthorized" or "undocumented" immigrant to mean the immigration status of people who do not have the federal documentation to show that they are legally entitled to work, visit or live in the United States (Passel 2006; see also U.S.CIS 2008). It is acknowledged, however, that the term "undocumented" immigrant is preferable in order to avoid what is perceived as stereotypical or degrading labeling of immigrants (see Stillwell 2006). As gathered from the interviews as well as from the literature review, the term "illegal alien" is commonly used to describe a foreign immigrant who (1) owes no allegiance to the United States; (2) whose mere presence in the United States is in violation of the law; and (3) who has violated a condition of a lawful entry (Chiswick 1997). From this perspective, he or she is, therefore, considered criminal under applicable U.S. laws. In this work, the term "illegal alien" is only used either as a direct citation or to express or refer to the opinion of anti-immigrant groups or individuals. In any case, it is always set in quotation marks to indicate that it does not express the author's opinion.

Neither the use of the terms "undocumented" or "unauthorized" nor the use of the word "illegal" are in any way intended to pass judgment of any kind.

PART II: THEORETICAL BACKGROUND

> On the border, a spectrum of different encounters presents a broad array of human interactions that reveal the richness of both cultures. [...] You can compare impressions with many different people from the other culture every day. To be at the border is to be on top of a fence that looks at two different lands that are neighbours. The border is also the place where ideologues impose their prejudice. Some Americans wanted to stop Mexicans from entering the United States because they thought they were drug dealers. They wanted to keep Mexicans away by militarizing the border. They built a high iron fence that many still believe stops illegal immigrants and drugs. In reality, the fence stops neither. But it is a symbolic gesture that makes sense to people motivated by prejudice against another culture, and as the pioneer sociologist W.I. Thomas said, when people define things as real, they become real in their consequences. But the border is also a place of accommodation between individuals. It is a place where people from both sides mix words from both languages to create a new language they can use to solve everyday problems.
>
> ~ Bustamante 1992: 486

3. Vigilantism

A review of academic literature indicates that there seems to be a good deal of consensus on the fact that vigilantism and a vigilante tradition exist (Brown 1975; Burrows 1976; Waldrep 1993; Moses 1997). Nonetheless, there appears to be no adequate theoretical framework from which to analyze this phenomenon (Rosenbaum & Sederberg 1976; Johnston 1996; Abrahams 1998). One reason for this is that the phenomenon itself is difficult to define because it "articulates to ever-changing social realities" (Pratten & Sen 2008: 19; see also Hine 1997), while the concept itself is rather "enigmatic" (Johnston 1996: 221). The phenomena this term represents are "multifaceted, emotionally highly charged and changeable" (Abrahams 1998: 4). Groups as diverse as anti-abortionists, state militias, opponents of disfavored politicians, unofficial protesters or even former British Prime Minister Tony Blair have been called "vigilantes" (Hine 1997; see also Abrahams 1998; Hall 2003).

The term "vigilante" has not always had the negative connotation that frequently accompanies its use today. Originally, "vigilante" was a Spanish word meaning "watchman" or "guard". It has its roots in the Latin word "vigil" which means to be awake or to be observant (Abrahams 1998). Nowadays, the word is seldom used in its original sense. More commonly, vigilantism is defined as "taking the law into one's own hands" (Brown 1976; Johnson 1981; Doty 2007; Pratten & Sen 2008) – a definition which tends to conjure up images of the American Wild West and of "rowdy cowboys lynching an unfortunate horse thief" (Rosenbaum & Sederberg 1976: 4). It is also referred to as "extra-legal force" or "extra-legal justice" (Fritz 1994), "violent self-help" (Hine 1997) or "extra-legal violence" (Brown 1976).

One of the first academic writers to research the vigilante phenomenon was historian Richard Maxwell Brown. In his book on the history of American violence and vigilantism he approaches vigilantism from a socio-legal perspective and attempts to define it by saying that it represents "morally sanctimonious behavior" aimed at rectifying or remedying a "structural flaw" in society (1975: 23), with the flaw usually being some place where the law is ineffective or not enforced. He sees vigilantism as being closely connected to America's frontier history and its revolutionary origins.

A different perspective is taken by Jon Rosenbaum and Peter Sederberg. As political scientists, they view vigilantism as a sub-category of political violence and define it simply as "establishment violence" consisting of "acts or threats of coercion in violation of the formal boundaries of an established socio-political order which, however, are intended by the violators to defend that order from some form of subversion" (Rosenbaum & Sederberg 1976: 4).

Les Johnston (1996) criticizes this approach as being over-inclusive. He argues that defining vigilantism as "establishment violence" produces a concept which describes such a wide range of heterogeneous behaviors that it "covers everything and, therefore, nothing" (1996: 222). This makes it "neither helpful to criminology nor specific enough to permit such operationalization as is necessary for empirical analysis" (Johnston 1996: 221). Instead, Johnston proposes a criminological definition of vigilantism based on six key features.

3.1 Johnston's Criminological Definition

According to Johnston (1996), vigilantism is a social movement giving rise to premeditated acts of force – or threatened force – by autonomous citizens. It arises as a reaction to the transgression of institutionalized norms by individuals or groups – or to their potential or imputed transgression, and its acts are focused upon crime control and/or social control. Finally, the movement also aims to offer assurances (or "guarantees") of security both to its participants and to other members of a given established order. Johnston's approach neither assumes vigilante activity to be extra-legal nor to involve the necessary imposition of punishment on victims.

It is the normative aspect in Johnston's definition which provides the initial justification for deeming vigilantism to be a criminological concept; and it is also this aspect that distinguishes vigilantism from mere "establishment violence".

However, the "key to understanding vigilantism" (Johnston 1996: 226) lies in Johnston's concept of "autonomous citizenship". In order for an act to qualify as vigilantism, it is crucial that the act constitute a voluntary activity engaged in by "active citizens" without the state's authority or any kind of state support and not for commercial purposes (Johnston

1996). This is what makes vigilantism different from "responsible" citizenship, such as, for example, neighborhood watches, which are recognized and authorized by the state, or private security personnel.

Table 1 Johnston's Six Key Features of Vigilantism

- It involves planning and premeditation by those engaging in it
- Its participants are private citizens whose engagement is voluntary
- It is a form of "autonomous" citizenship and, as such, constitutes a social movement
- It uses or threatens the use of force
- It arises when an established order is under threat from the transgression, the potential transgression, or the imputed transgression of institutionalized norms
- It aims to control crime or other social infractions by offering assurances (or "guarantees") of security both to participants and to others

Source: Johnston 1996: 222 – 232.

For the remainder of this book, this definition provides the theoretical framework from which to approach the emergence of the MCDC as a vigilante phenomenon.

3.2 Delineations

Related to vigilantism have been other movements of extra-legal violence, such as the Ku Klux Klan (see Brown 1976), paramilitary organizations (see Lutterbeck 2004), guerrilla movements (see Huggins 1991), social bandits (see Hobsbawm 1959), militias (see Freilich et al. 2001) or various types of self-help (see Abrahams 1998). Ray Abrahams even treats death squads and mafias as one form of vigilantism, although he admits that including them "pushes the concept of vigilantism to its limits" (Abrahams 1998: 136; see also Huggins 1991). What makes these groups so similar to vigilantism - and thus more or less difficult to delineate from it - is that all of these

> typically involve groups that operate within or on the edge of society and constitute an (often enough violent) alternative to the institutions of the formal political and economic sectors. All are also commonly engaged, either among themselves or more widely, in one or other form of social control, and they all lay claim to some constituency of support (Abrahams 1998: 163).

Nevertheless, some differences do exist. For example, self-help differs conceptually from vigilantism in that it generally takes place between structurally equal individuals or groups and is mostly spontaneous (Abrahams 1998). Vigilantism, on the other hand, involves planning and premeditation by those engaging in it (Johnston 1996). Paramilitaries and death squads tend to be either composed of police and/or military personnel or at least tied to state security (Huggins 1991; Abrahams 1998; Lutterbeck 2004).[4] Often times these groups carry out the extra-judicial extermination of a variety of people who have been defined as "public enemies" and "undesirables" by the state (Abrahams 1998) - something which contradicts Johnston's concept of "autonomous citizenship". Finally, a difference can also be found in the aims and motives of those engaging in this kind of activity. Whereas some of these movements resort to force in order to overthrow the established order and create new arrangements, vigilantes seek to restore order and maintain the status quo (Johnston 1996; Rosenbaum & Sederberg 1976; Abrahams 1998; Chacón & Davis 2007).

---

[4] Whereas Rosenbaum & Sederberg acknowledge the existence of "official" vigilantism and include acts by public (off-duty and on-duty) police officers in their definition, Johnston calls this inclusion "dubious" (1996: 224). He argues that police officers continue to enjoy full police powers whether they are on-duty or not; even their off-duty actions cannot be demarcated from their public status, functions, and responsibilities. On a conceptual level, he says, including the acts of public officers "misconceives the nature of police operational practice" (Johnston 1996: 224).

4. The Emergence of Vigilantism

Rosenbaum and Sederberg (1976) differentiate between three basic types of vigilantism, depending on the intended purpose of the vigilante action: crime control vigilantism, social-group control vigilantism and regime control vigilantism.

Crime control vigilantism encompasses violence "directed against people believed to be committing acts proscribed by the formal legal system, which harm private persons or property" (Rosenbaum & Sederberg 1976: 10). It aims at restoring law and order. Social-group vigilantism constitutes violence "directed against groups that are competing for, or advocating a redistribution of, values within the system" (Rosenbaum & Sederberg 1976: 12). Its primary purpose is to preserve the status quo. The third basic type of vigilantism intends to alter the "regime" itself so as to turn it into a more effective guardian of the "base" (Rosenbaum & Sederberg 1976: 17).

Similarly, Johnston (1996) distinguishes between two modes of vigilantism: one focusing on crime control and the other focusing on social control (though he does not consider these two to be mutually exclusive).

These typologies not only reveal something about the intentions of vigilantes, but also about the social context of vigilantism and, thus, about the circumstances under which it might emerge. It appears that the potential for vigilantism exists where certain groups in society believe that they possess a vested interest in the preservation of the current distribution of values but perceive that established order to be under threat (Rosenbaum & Sederberg 1976; see also Fritz 1994; Johnston 1996; Jacobs 2005). Once the "establishment" is perceived as threatened – either through crime or social mobility – and the government fails to satisfactorily control those who pose the threat, vigilantism is said to emerge:

> Vigilantism [...] often constitutes a criticism of the failure of state machinery to meet the felt needs of those who resort to it. It is a form of self-help, with varying degrees of violence, which is activated instead of such machinery, against criminals and others whom the actors perceive as

undesirables, deviants and "public enemies" (Abrahams 1998: 9).

When normally citizens successfully depend on the state to deal with criminals and other challenges to the prevailing socio-political order, in "vigilante mode" (Abrahams 1998: 8) citizens lay claim, at least temporarily, to the state's own mantle of authority and try to deal directly with those whom they regard as threatening (see also Chacón & Davis 2007).

Figure 1 Structure of Relations between "Good" Citizens, Criminals and the State

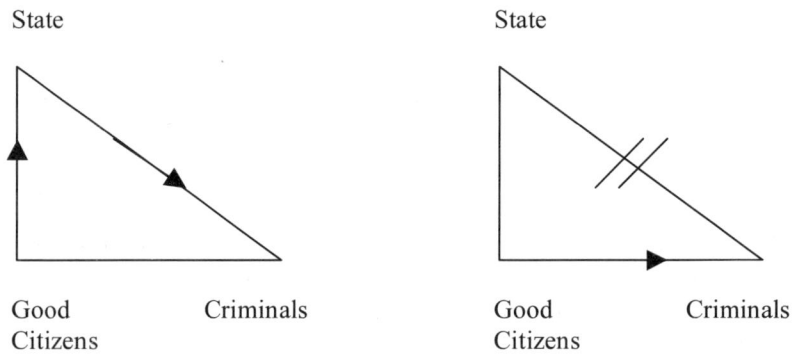

Source: Abrahams 1998: 8.

According to Johnston (1996), the motivation for much vigilante action arises from such a popular desire to "do something," however unrealistic, to ensure that the established system of order prevails.[5] Typically, so Johnston, vigilantes will try to control these threats by offering assurances (or "guarantees") of security.

---

[5] Of course, as Abrahams rightly remarks, vigilantism's tendency to arise in real or alleged social and political crises also provides it with "special opportunities to conceal a variety of purposes behind assertions of public spirit, moral rectitude and the need for desperate measures in a desperate situation" (1998: 22).

5. Immigration Control and Security

Security is almost as an "elusive" (Weiner 1995: 145) and "paradoxical" (Johnston 1996: 230) concept as vigilantism. Customarily, the word "security" is located beside the word "threat" (Beare 1999; Smith 2005). This also highlights the essentially negative character of security: it exists when something does not occur. Security, therefore, can be seen as the "absence" of threat to acquired values and, in a subjective sense, as the absence of fear that anything occurs which threatens or alters the established status quo (Johnston 1996; Weiner 1995; Smith 2005); but, as Johnston writes, because peace is "seldom something that simply happens" (1996: 231) *assurances* of security are required. Which "assurances" successfully restore order and control, depends on the nature of the threat itself.

Traditionally, security thinking and analysis have been dominated by two broad categories of threats: challenges to a state's internal security and threats to its external security (Lutterbeck 2004; Smith 2005; Kirchner 2007; Dauvergne 2007). While internal security has been understood in terms of criminal or otherwise disturbing activities within the boundaries of the state, threats to external security have been considered to arise mainly due to aggression by other states (Krahmann 2003; Lutterbeck 2004; Kirchner 2007).

Since the end of the Cold War, threats have generally become more social in nature (Lutterbeck 2004; Kirchner 2007). There seems to be relatively broad agreement among scholars that the main risks facing countries today are non-state and transnational, consisting of various illicit or uncontrolled cross-border phenomena, rather than state-based (see Buzan 1991; Johnston 1996; Lutterbeck 2004; Booth 2005). While formerly threats targeted the state's ability to govern, these new security threats are generally aimed at society and are seen as threatening the social contract (see Kirchner 2007). At the top of this "new security agenda," one typically finds such issues as drug trafficking, human smuggling or undocumented immigration (see Lutterbeck 2004; Doty 1998; Krahmann 2003; Caparini & Marenin 2006). Still, there is no single criterion that determines what social conditions will be labeled a threat or a security issue.

In the migration realm, therefore, Catherine Dauvergne (2007) suggests using a constructivist approach as it can help to understand the intransigence of debates over migration and security. The constructivist approach focuses on "how states, nations, people or others come to understand something as an important threat to their existence or way of being" (Dauvergne 2007: 542). Once this is understood, so Dauvergne, the approach can also help to understand the sometimes extraordinary actions (suspending or circumventing what counts as "normal" decision-making) that people take in response to these perceived threats.

One way that security is constructed is by means of a process called "securitization". In fact, immigration has become one of the most prominent issues being securitized today (see Zimmermann 1995; Doty 2007; Bosworth 2008; Walters 2008).

5.1 Defining "Securitization"

Securitization is the "process through which the definition and understanding of a particular phenomenon, its consequences, and the policies/courses of action deemed appropriate to address the issue are subjected to a particular logic" (Doty 1998: 71). According to Barry Buzan et al. (1998), three requirements must be met in order for an issue to be securitized:

First, there must be a referent object, that is, something that is seen to be existentially threatened. What constitutes the "threat" is heavily dependent on the particular character of the referent object in question (Kirchner 2007; see also Emmers 2007). Here Buzan et al. (1998) differentiate between different sectors in society (military, political, economic, social and environmental). For example, in the political sector "sovereignty" can be the referent object which can be existentially threatened by anything that questions recognition, legitimacy, or governing authority (Buzan et al. 1998).

Secondly, there must be a securitizing actor (or several actors) who securitizes the issue by declaring the referent object to be existentially threatened. It is in this practice that the issue becomes a security issue – "not necessarily because a real existential threat exists but because the issue is presented as such a threat" (Buzan et al. 1998: 24; see also Dauvergne 2007; Emmers 2007). Once the issue has been presented as existentially threatened, the securitizing actor can argue that it is more important than other issues, and that it should take absolute priority on the political agenda. Furthermore, by labeling the issue a "security" issue, the actor can claim the need for and the right to treat it by extraordinary means. The invocation of security is, thus, in a sense the key to legitimizing the use of force; and it opens the way for the state to mobilize, or to take special powers, to handle existential threats (Buzan et al. 1998).

The securitizing actor does not always have to be the state. It is "possible for other social entities to raise an issue to the level of general consideration or even to the status of sanctioned urgency among themselves" (Buzan et al. 1998: 24). This means that securitization of an issue can originate from varied and dispersed locales (see also Doty 1998; Emmers 2007). Also, whether an issue is a security issue is not something individuals decide alone.

Lastly, an issue is only successfully securitized if and when the audience accepts it as such (Buzan et al. 1998). This is the case when the issue has been argued and has gained enough resonance "for a platform to be made from which it is possible to legitimize emergency measures...that would not have been possible had the discourse not taken the form of existential threats" (Buzan et al. 1998: 25).

5.2 "Securitization" and Immigration

Three different modes of securitization can be found in contemporary discourses with regard to immigration. Each mode is driven by a specific security logic and is associated with a particular type of politics which in turn gives rise to certain policy possibilities (Doty 1998).

National security mode focuses on the security of the nation-state as an entity. Security in this mode is defined in political/military terms as the protection of the boundaries and integrity of the state and its values (Doty 1998; see also Andreas & Price 2001; Krahmann 2003; Smith 2005; Kirchner 2007). An issue is securitized when it is understood as a threat or potential threat to the stability or survival of the state (Doty 2007; see also Mabee 2003; Smith 2005; Roe 2007). The result is that immigration comes "to be seen as [an invasion] necessitating strategic action along the lines of more traditional threats to national security" (Doty 1998: 77).

In societal security mode, the referent object is society and not the state. What is threatened in this mode is not so much the state but identity, "the ability of a society to persist in its essential character under changing conditions and possible or actual threats" (Doty 1998: 77; see also Waever 1995; Roe 2007). In societal security mode, any legislation passed will attempt to reassert the identity of those who belong to this particular society, while simultaneously defining those who will be excluded (Waever 1995; Doty 1998; Roe 2007).

Human security mode emphasizes the security of people as human beings (Altvater 2003; Kerr 2007). The referent object in this mode is the individual person, and what is at stake is each individual's personal security. As a result of this logic, immigration might not be seen as a threat because "one's identity would not be threatened by the presence of an unrecognizable and inassimilable other" (Doty 1998: 83).

For the purpose of this project, each one of these three modes could help to understand how threats and security – as "modes of self-defense and national interest" – are being discursively deployed by the MCDC to securitize the U.S. – Mexico border as a "conduit for terrorist and migrant incursions" (Ackleson 2005: 180). However, this project focuses on national security mode as the one that has been linked most directly to the emergence of the Minutemen.

6. The Historical and Legal Context of American Vigilantism

The emergence of vigilantism cannot be understood without taking into account its social, cultural and historical context (Abrahams 1998; see also Chavez 2008; Pratten & Sen 2008). In fact, Pratten and Sen suggest that "long historical trajectories and particular cultural repertoires are the proximate and pressing imperatives behind vigilante violence" (2008: 5).

David Kowalewski (1996) similarly highlights the importance of looking at the historical context when he proposes that a history of vigilantism in a country predisposes it to vigilantism in the present; and Brown (1975) has identified several key elements in American society and culture that, he claims, can explain America's long-standing vigilante tradition. Brown (1975) argues that, *inter alia*, the country's revolutionary origins, its history and ideology of the "frontier," the idea of "popular sovereignty," and its asserted right of citizens to carry arms and to defend themselves, are all elements which have turned the United States into a country so prone to vigilante activity.[6]

Moreover, the United States and Mexico share a distinctive history that not only makes Mexican immigration different from all other immigration, but also creates a unique atmosphere in the border region. Some scholars even directly attribute the origin of many contemporary border issues and problems to this history (see e.g. Jamail 1981). In this chapter, these unique historical and legal aspects are discussed.

6.1 Vigilantism in United States History

The history of vigilantism in the United States is as old as the country itself (see Caughey 1960; Brown 1975; Burrows 1976; Marx & Archer 1976; Waldrep 1993; Moses 1997). In many ways, the history of the United States began with vigilantism. From the first major outbreak of

---

[6] The fact that America's vigilante history still has a strong impact on American society today, especially when it comes to the use of violence, is underscored by Jacobs' 2005 study of vigilantism and the death penalty. In this study, Jacobs found that death sentences were most likely in states with large minority populations that also had a history of frequent vigilante violence. He believes that this is the case because the death sentence today is regarded as a legal and, therefore, more acceptable replacement for former lynching and other vigilante activities.

vigilantism in the United States during the Regulator movement of the South Carolina back country from 1767 to 1769, to the San Francisco Vigilance Committees in 1851/1856, or the Associated Farmers during the Great Depression, vigilante movements have played an integral part in American history and culture (Brown 1975; see also Marx & Archer 1976; Fritz 1994; Abrahams 1998; Chacón & Davis 2007). Whenever "people felt that there was too much crime, that their persons or property were in danger, that cherished traditions and values were being threatened, and that regular law-enforcement officials were not coping with the problem, vigilante-type efforts frequently emerged" (Marx & Archer 1976: 130). From 1767 to 1951 "there were at least 326 vigilante movements or episodes distributed over practically all of the trans-Appalachian states and a few of the Atlantic states" (Brown 1975: 79); many of these movements were violent. Kelly Hine (1997) differentiates between three distinct incarnations of vigilantism in American history: classical vigilantism, neo-vigilantism, and pseudo-vigilantism.

Classical vigilantism originated during the late colonial or early federal period and concerned itself primarily with policing deviants on the expanding western frontier (Hine 1997). For this reason, this form of vigilantism is often referred to as "essentially a frontier phenomenon" (Abrahams 1998: 2). As the American frontier expanded rapidly, the effectiveness of state power typically spread unevenly over the state's territory (Brown 1975; Abrahams 1998). Absent more civilized legal controls, the people living in those frontier regions are said to have frequently resorted to extra-legal violence to restore order:

> A vigilante roundup of ne'er-do-wells and outlaws followed by their flogging, expulsion, or killing, not only solved the problem of disorder, but also had crucial symbolic value as well. Vigilante action was a clear warning to disorderly inhabitants that the newness of settlement would provide no opportunity to erode the established framework of civilization. Vigilantism was a violent sanctification of the deeply cherished values of life and property (Brown 1976:81).

Though most of these early vigilante movements did involve violence, it was not always necessary for a powerful movement to take a large number of lives. Often a vigilante movement could achieve its aims by executing just a few persons or even only one (Brown 1976: 87).

Some of the "outlaws and marginal types" (Brown 1975: 97) taken up by vigilantes were given formal (though illegal) trials in which the accused had an opportunity to defend themselves (see Caughey 1960; Brown 1975; Johnson 1981). If they were thought hopelessly incorrigible, they were either driven from the area, forced to work on the plantations, or subjected to one of three punishments: branding, whipping or hanging (Brown 1975).

The second type of vigilantism, neo-vigilantism, arose in San Francisco in the mid-1850s. Whereas classical vigilantism arose because of a lack of established law enforcement systems, this type of vigilantism emerged where regular police and a legal system were already functioning, but where alien groups were seen to threaten the established order (Brown 1975; see also Marx & Archer 1976; Hine 1997; Doty 2007). The San Francisco vigilance committee of 1856 is probably the most famous of these neo-vigilante movements. It is often called the "largest and most influential vigilante group in American history" (Fritz 1994: 58), and it has had a tremendous impact on American vigilantism (see Marx & Archer 1976; Abrahams 1998; Chacón & Davis 2007). What made the 1856 Committee so unique was the fact that it had more than 8,000 reputed members, that it was controlled by the city's most prominent merchants, and that it was organized in a paramilitary fashion (Johnson 1981). In addition, their motivation was different: these vigilantes did not just want to punish criminals; they wanted to overturn existing political and judicial institutions and to install a new order (Johnson 1981). In order to achieve these goals, they turned the vigilance committee into a political party that dominated urban politics for almost ten years (Brown 1975; Johnson 1981; Chacón & Davis 2007). The San Francisco example is, thus, "one in which a struggle for political power masquerades as a vigilante movement, vigilantism arising not from crime but from an orchestrated moral panic about crime" (Johnson 1981: 229). While the effects of earlier movements were "temporary and superficial," those of the 1856 committee were "radical and permanent" (Johnson 1981: 583).

The third type of vigilantism, pseudo-vigilantism, refers to vigilante groups which surfaced following the dramatic increases in crime and the social upheavals experienced in the 1960s (Johnston 1996; Hine 1997; see also Mandel 2001). This type of vigilantism combines traits of both its predecessors. Some of the first civilian border patrol groups, like the Hanigans[7] in 1976 or the *Civilian Materiel Assistance*[8] in 1986, which began to appear along the U.S. – Mexico border at that time, are examples of such pseudo-vigilante movements (Conover 1997; Moser 2006; Doty 2007; Walker 2007).

Clearly, as the economic and social profile of the United States changed over the centuries, the character of vigilantism also changed, but the phenomenon itself never quite disappeared. Until today, America's history seems inextricably entwined with the history of vigilantism and vice versa. In fact, the idea of "violent self-help" has very much become part of American culture and it is often not only tolerated, but also promoted "as necessary and beneficial conduct" (Hine 1997: 1223). Any scholar studying a contemporary form of vigilantism in the United States, therefore, cannot do this without bearing in mind the historical and cultural significance of this phenomenon.

6.2 Vigilantism and the Law

Although the character of vigilantism has changed over time, one aspect of it has remained the same: its seemingly paradoxical relationship with the law. However, whether or not it appears paradoxical to try to "uphold

---

[7] In 1976, three Mexican nationals crossed the border fence into Cochise County and were heading for nearby job sites, when they stopped to re-fill their water jug. At that time, they were taken hostage at gun-point by rancher Tom Hanigan, who was later joined by his father and brother. The three men threatened and tortured the three Mexicans for hours. When the Hanigans decided to let them go, "they cut them free one at a time, pointing them to Mexico and opening fire with birdshot" (Moser 2006: 142). The Mexicans somehow survived and reported the incident to officials.
[8] The *Civilian Materiel Assistance* is a paramilitary group that is said to have had ties to the contras in Nicaragua. In 1986, they reportedly detained immigrants at gun-point, threatened and assaulted them before turning them over to Border Patrol.

the law by breaking the law," depends on one's view of the nature of law itself (Abrahams 1998). Aside from looking at history then, several legal doctrines are of relevance when it comes to understanding why "violent self-help" has so frequently emerged in the United States, and why it was able to become such an integral part of American culture. The most important of these doctrines is the idea of popular sovereignty. In addition, the constitutionally protected right of citizens to carry arms and to defend themselves, contemporary citizen's arrest statutes, and the Constitution's Invasion Clause are of relevance and will be outlined briefly.

6.2.1 Popular Sovereignty

Popular sovereignty is the notion that no law or rule is legitimate unless it directly or indirectly rests on the consent of the people concerned. It is "the people" who are the ultimate and only legitimate basis for government. Only "the people"[9] possess the right to reform, alter, or abolish their government at any time (Culberson 1990; see also Fritz 1994; Yack 2001; Axtmann 2004). This doctrine dates back to the founding days of the United States and provides the principle rationale for vigilante activities (Brown 1975; Fritz 1994; Doty 2007). Indeed, vigilantism is often regarded as the romanticized idea of a temporary embodiment of popular sovereignty (Johnston 1981).

An excerpt from an 1858 resolution of a group of northern Indiana vigilantes nicely illustrates the connection between vigilantism and popular sovereignty, as well as the instrumental understanding of law prevalent in American society in general:[10]

> We are believers in the doctrine of popular sovereignty; that the people of this country are the real sovereign, and that whenever the laws, made by

---

[9] Who is meant by the term "the people" is somewhat disputed. There seems to be some consensus, however, that it does not refer to the majority of citizens but rather to the people as the sum of legally equal citizens or as a political community (see Abrahams 1998; Yack, 2001; Axtmann 2004; see also U.S. Supreme Court in District of Columbia v. Heller (2008)).

[10] Brown writes that the answer to the apparent contradiction between lawfulness and disregard for laws "lies in the selectivity with which American have approached the law…[They have] a tendency to obey only such laws as they chose to obey…laws which did not suit the people were disobeyed" (1975: 132).

> those to whom they have delegated their authority, are found inadequate to their protection, it is the right of the people to take the protection of their property into their own hands, and deal with these villains according to their just deserts... (quoted in Brown 1975: 95).

Based on the notion that the law is made "by the people for the people," vigilantes not only believe that it is their right, but also their duty, to fend for themselves and to enforce the law if the government fails to do so. For them this right is a form of self-preservation which flows naturally from the ideals of popular sovereignty (Brown 1975; see also Hine 1997). Vigilantism is deemed a rightful action of "good citizens" (Abrahams 1998).

6.2.2 Self-Preservation and the Right to Bear Arms

Self-preservation is considered to be a fundamental right and "the first law of nature" (Brown 1975: 116). It follows from this that, although state and federal governments are usually given what amounts to a monopoly over the use of force, if necessary, private citizens may use force when their own life or property or the life of another are in danger. In this regard, the inherent right of self-defense is central to the right of citizens to carry arms.[11]

The right to bear arms is granted to American citizens under the Second Amendment of the U.S. Constitution, which reads as follows:

> A well regulated Militia, being necessary to the security of a free State, the right of the people to keep and bear Arms, shall not be infringed.

Originally, it is said to have been intended to protect the people from government tyranny (see Levinson 2002). Nowadays, the right to bear arms is becoming ever more important in a "highly threatening environment" in which citizens believe that "they need to provide their own security [...] because the government is unable or unwilling to do so"

---

[11] In Beard v. U.S. (1895), the Supreme Court approved the common-law-rule that a person "may repel force by force" in self-defense, and concluded that, when attacked, a person "is entitled to stand his ground and meet any attack made upon him with a deadly weapon".

(Mandel 2001: 130). This development is reflected in a recent decision by the U.S. Supreme Court. While for a long time it was controversial whether the word "militia" in this Amendment referred to the states' right to organize their own militias or to the right of the individual citizen to carry a weapon for his protection (see Levinson 2002), in <u>District of Columbia v. Heller</u> (2008) the Supreme Court now ruled that the Second Amendment protects a purely individual right.[12]

6.2.3 Citizens' Arrest Statutes

Another frequently cited legal basis for vigilante activities, especially with regard to border-patrolling activities, are the so-called citizens' arrest statutes.

Citizens' arrest statutes grant ordinary citizens the right to detain persons suspected of having committed a crime. With the exception of North Carolina[13], all states in the United States have citizens' arrest statutes, but their exact provisions vary from state to state. As is the case with self-defense, the circumstances under which the law authorizes private individuals to make arrests are very narrow. Generally, citizens are only permitted to make arrests for crimes committed in their presence. Some jurisdictions even limit these crimes to felonies and breaches of the peace (see Paris 2002). Such is the case in Arizona, which is the focus of this research, and it is therefore relevant to briefly outline this particular citizen arrest statute.

In the state of Arizona, a private person may make an arrest only when (a) "the person to be arrested has in his presence committed a misdemeanour amounting to a breach of the peace," or (b) "a felony has been in fact committed and he has reasonable ground to believe that the person to be arrested has committed it" (Ariz. Rev. Stat. Ann. §13-3884: 2008). For the case of immigration, this means that citizens may only lawfully detain illegal immigrants at the border if "unlawful entry"[14] into the

---

[12] <u>District of Columbia v. Heller</u> (2008).

[13] North Carolina has citizens' detention laws.

[14] "Unlawful entry" is the act of unlawfully crossing the United States border. It is defined broadly under federal law to include "any alien" who: (1) "enters or attempts to enter the United States at any time or place other than as designated by immigration officers," or (2) "eludes examination or inspection by immigra-

United States qualifies as either a felony or a misdemeanor amounting to a "breach of the peace." However, crossing the border without proper documentation is not a felony for the first attempt (§275 (a) INA; 8 U.S.C. §1325 and §1326; see also Walker 2007: 156). Only if the migrant attempts to re-enter into the United States after he has been removed once, does his entry constitute a felony crime[15], and a vigilante has no way of knowing whether this is the migrant's first or second attempt at crossing the border. That unlawful entry qualifies as a misdemeanor amounting to a "breach of the peace" is also rather unlikely (see Walker 2007).[16]

Therefore, despite the existence of these statutes, vigilante groups patrolling the border face potentially serious legal problems if, in carrying out their activities, they hold, detain or subdue one of the migrants. If they do make an unlawful arrest, they can be charged with false imprisonment or even kidnapping. In addition, they can be further penalized under state law depending on whether unreasonable force or unreasonable

---

tion officers," or (3) "attempts to enter or obtains entry into the United States by a willfully false or misleading representation or the willful concealment of a material fact". Undocumented migrants can be fined or imprisoned up to six months for their first unlawful entry (§275(a) INA; 8 U.S.C. §1325(a) (2008)).

[15] Attempts have been made in the past to change the law so that already the first attempt at border-crossing would constitute a felony. For example, the *Antiterrorism and Illegal Immigration Control Act*, which was passed by the House in 2005 but was struck down in the Senate, would have further criminalized undocumented border-crossing as a felony (see *Antiterrorism and Illegal Immigration Control Act*, H.R. 4437, 109th Cong. (2005); see also Garcia 2006; Walker 2007). Similarly, Arizona State Legislature passed a law in 2006 that would have allowed the arrest and prosecution of undocumented migrants under Arizona's trespassing law. However, the bill was vetoed by the governor.

[16] Arizona has not explicitly defined "breach of the peace". Arizona law merely includes a "disorderly conduct" statute, which prohibits any fighting, making loud noises, using profane language or gestures, or recklessly displaying a deadly weapon with "intent to disturb the peace" (Ariz. Rev. Stat. Ann. §13-2904 (a) (2008)). Although "breach of the peace" is not limited to behaviour prohibited by the disorderly conduct statute (see State v. Chavez, 96 P.3d 1093 (Ariz. Ct. App. 2004); Williams v. Sup. Ct. of Pima Cty., 512 P.2d 45 (Ariz. Ct. App. 1973)), Walker (2007) considers it highly unlikely that under the majority rule unlawful entry would be considered as such. Past legislation indicates otherwise, he argues.

delay was used before delivering the offender to a law enforcement officer (see Ariz. Rev. Stat. Ann. §13-1303 and §13-3900: 2008).

6.2.4 The Invasion-Clause

One final legal justification which some vigilante groups put forward – and this is more of an argument pertaining to groups along the U.S. – Mexico border in particular – is that the United States is being invaded by Mexican immigrants and that this "foreign invasion"[17] must be stopped (see Hayworth 2006; Gilchrist & Corsi 2006; Doty 2007). This argument relates again to the inherent right to self-defense discussed earlier and to the understanding that self-defense is intrinsic to the concept of sovereignty (see Levinson 2002; Glon 2004). Sovereignty is considered its own justification for taking measures in self-defense. This means that nations may use self-defense in order to protect their territory and citizens as long as they do not infringe upon the territorial integrity or political independence of other nations (Glon 2004).

Over the last couple of years, the total immigrant population (legal and illegal) in the United States has reached record numbers, and it is projected to grow even more over the next couple of years; by 2050, one in five Americans (19%) is projected to be foreign-born.[18] In 2008, 12.7 million of the total immigrant population was estimated to be immigrants from Mexico. This means that Mexican immigrants account for about

---

[17] See e.g.: www.desertinvasion.us/info/background.html; see also
http://www.americanborderpatrol.com/;
http://chicagominutemanproject.com/aboutus.html;
http://www.americanminutemen.org; http://www.noinvaders.org/home.shtml;
http://www.theamericanresistance.com/index.html; http://www.alipac.us/; all sites last visited on 11 September 2008.

[18] "If present trends continue, within two decades the foreign-born population of the United States will surpass the historic 19th-century peak of nearly 15 percent of all residents [...]," reported a *New York Times* article on 2 November 2008 (see Roberts 2008). And the *Pew Research Center* finds that: "If current trends continue, the population of the United States will rise to 438 million in 2050, from 296 million in 2005, and 82% of the increase will be due to immigrants arriving from 2005 to 2050 and their U.S.-born descendants." As of July 2009, the United States has an estimated total population of 307,212,123 (see CIA World Factbook 2009).

32% of all immigrants living in the country; more than any other group of immigrants in the United States. It also means that, as *Pew Hispanic Center*'s Jeffrey Passel ominously points out, already more than "10 percent of the Mexican-born population [are] in the United States with less than 90 percent in Mexico" (2004).[19]

Mexicans are also said to comprise more than half of all unauthorized immigrants in the United States (see Nuscheler 2004; Rosas 2006, Camarota 2007; Batalova 2008; Hoefer at al. 2009). A study conducted by the *Pew Research Center* estimates that Mexicans make up about six-in-ten, or 59%, of the estimated 11.9 million unauthorized immigrants living in the United States.[20] In addition, anti-immigrant groups speak of an average of 10,000 or more unauthorized immigrants crossing the border every day (see Gilchrist & Corsi 2006; see also e.g. Desert Invasion 2008; Project USA 2008; American Border Patrol 2008). These figures make Mexico not only the largest source of legal immigration to the United States, but also the single largest source of unauthorized immigration (see Passel 2004; Walker 2007; Hoefer et al. 2009).

What is more, scholars like Gilberto Rosas argue that the "borderlands condition is 'thickening'" (2006: 344), meaning that it is migrating across the United States from its origin in the south-western borderlands. While Mexican immigrants are still settling in "traditional" destination states like California and Texas, since the late 1990s, immigrants from Mexico, like other immigrant groups, have begun moving to "non-traditional" settlement areas, such as Georgia, North Carolina, or even Nebraska and Ohio (see Huntington 2004; Hayworth 2006; Batalova 2008).[21] Altogether, the Mexican immigrant population outside the four

---

[19] As of July 2009, Mexico's estimated total population is 111,211,789 (see CIA World Factbook 2009).
[20] For more information on how these estimates are calculated using the "residual" methodology and on possible limitations of these numbers, see Hoefer et al. 2009.
[21] Based on data provided by Passel (2004), the share of Mexican immigrants residing in the four traditional states (CA, TX, IL, AZ) states has dropped from 89 percent in 1990 to 72 percent in 2002. Passel attributes this decrease to the fact that Mexican immigrants have moved out of these states, especially California, both to nearby states and to totally new settlement areas in other parts of the country: "The share of new immigrants from Mexico going to these non-traditional settlement areas greatly increased. Mexican immigrants moved to the

largest states (California, Texas, Illinois and Arizona) has increased more than five-fold between 1990 and 2002 from about 500,000 to 2.7 million (see Passel 2004).

These developments are the reason why many of the anti-immigrant groups in the United States are raising alarm. Unless immigration is controlled and the southern border is sealed off, they fear that:

> [...] just around the corner, whites in America are going to be disempowered...through a radical and rapid transformation of the nation's demography on a scale unprecedented in world history (Project USA 2008).

Even scholars like Samuel P. Huntington advocate this idea of an "invasion" and thereby only add fuel to the flames:

> The invasion of over 1 million Mexican civilians is a comparable threat [as 1 million Mexican soldiers] to American societal security, and Americans should react against it with comparable vigour. Mexican immigration looms as a unique and disturbing challenge to our cultural integrity, our national identity, and potentially our future as a country (2000:33).

The vigilante organizations regard the federal government as having a duty to protect the nation from such an "invasion" (see Glon 2004; Hayworth 2006; Doty 2007; Walker 2007). This "duty" is said to arise out of Article 4, §4 of the United States Constitution, which provides as follows:

> The United States... shall protect each of ... [the states] against Invasion.

---

south-eastern part of the country, including Alabama, Arkansas, Georgia, Kentucky, Mississippi, North Carolina, South Carolina, and Tennessee, for jobs in poultry processing, light manufacturing, and construction. In the upper Midwest, including Iowa, Nebraska, Minnesota, and Wisconsin, Mexican immigrants took jobs in pork, beef, and turkey processing. Two additional southern states, Delaware and Maryland, and the western states of Colorado and Utah, also experienced rapid growth in their Mexican-born populations between 1990 and 2000" (Passel 2004).

This clause is commonly referred to as the "Invasion Clause". In reference to this clause, the vigilante groups feel strongly that, although "ranches, border towns and public lands are being overrun as danger escalates" (Desert Invasion 2008) and "millions of illegal aliens and drug runners have entered into our nation" (Desert Invasion 2008), the federal government, "the very entity responsible for the tidal wave of illegal aliens entering our nation" (Desert Invasion 2008), fails to take adequate action to protect the country. They see the government as "more concerned with protecting the borders of countries half way around the world" (MCDC 2008; see also McGirk 2000) than its own border, and

> [e]ven when these illegal immigrants openly defy our laws and our sovereignty by displaying the Mexican flag and angrily proclaiming that California belongs to Mexico, we continue to let them stay (Gilchrist & Corsi 2006: 43).

For this reason, and because they don't want "our nation [to] drown under the weight of the needs, wants, and demands of illegal aliens" (Gilchrist & Corsi 2006: xx), the vigilante organizations argue that they must take the law into their own hands to enforce existing immigration laws and to protect America's southern border from this "invasion".

As suggested by the aforementioned quote from Jim Gilchrist and Jerome R. Corsi, sometimes this fear of a Mexican "invasion" also goes hand in hand with the fear of a Mexican *"reconquista,"* a supposed plot on the part of Mexico to retake the south-western United States, which has its origin in the history of the border itself (see also Tancredo 2006; Horwitz 2006; Doty 2007).

6.3 The Significance of the U.S. – Mexican Border

Almost all of Texas, New Mexico, Arizona, California, Nevada and Utah were part of Mexico, until Mexico sold these lands for $15 million to the United States in the wake of the Texan War of Independence (1835-1836) and the Mexican – American War (1846-1848). In 1848, Mexico ended the war when it signed the *Treaty of Guadalupe Hidalgo* and, thereby, established the current U.S. – Mexican border (Zinn 1999; Rodriguez 2006).

The aggressive expansion of the United States into Mexican territory at that time was to a large extent driven by the belief in "manifest destiny"[22] and the idea that the United States would be giving the blessings of liberty and democracy to more people (Chacón & Davis 2007). This was intermingled with "ideas of racial superiority, longings for the beautiful lands of New Mexico and California, and thoughts of commercial enterprise across the Pacific" (Zinn 1999: 154); sentiments which Milton Jamail (1981) regards as ever since having been reflected in the dominating stance which the United States has maintained toward Mexico. This tradition of conquest and dominance, he writes, has created a constant undercurrent of tension in the relationship between Mexico and the United States, and it has "nurtured a deeply felt spirit of mutual mistrust and antagonism" (Jamail 1981: 82). It has also made Mexican immigration different from all other immigration to the United States (Jamail 1981; see also Alvarez 1994; Huntington 2004; Tancredo 2006; Rodriguez 2006).[23]

Today, the nearly 2,000 mile boundary between the United States and Mexico separates one of the "most highly industrialized, technically advanced countries in the world from a developing country" (Jamail 1981: 78; see also Bustamante 1992; Glon 2004; Tancredo 2006; Romero 2008). It spans four U.S. states (New Mexico, Arizona, Texas and California) and six Mexican states (Baja California, Sonora, Chihuahua, Coahuila, Nuevo León, and Tamaulipas). This makes the border the ninth longest in the world and fourth longest in the Americas. It is a "gigantic…border, which is not only lines on a map but a complex labyrinth of

---

[22] The belief that the United States was destined by Providence to expand from the Atlantic to the Pacific.

[23] According to Huntington (2004), there are three main reasons why Mexican immigration can be considered to be different from all other immigration. First of all, no other immigrant group in American history has been able to assert a historical claim to American territory. Even today, 25 Mexican communities are still present in the United States, which have existed continuously since before the American conquest. Secondly, Mexicans arrive from a neighbouring country that "has suffered military defeat at the hands of the United States" (Huntington 2004: 233). Lastly, contiguity encourages Mexican immigration in particular because the costs and challenges of immigration for Mexicans are less than for other immigrant groups and they do not have to cut ties with the nation they left behind (see also Tancredo 2006).

entry points, status, intention, and time" (Tirman 2004: 7). There is "no other border in the world [that] exhibits the inequality of power, economics, and the human condition as does this one" (Alvarez 1995: 451; see also Ruiz 2006; Romero 2008).

Given these differing political economies and the border's distinct history of conquest and domination, it is no surprise that migration, especially in the U.S. – Mexican border region, lays at the heart of debates about national, social and economic policy, and national security (Ruiz 2006). Under circumstances like these, imposed and artificial boundaries, such as the one which divides the United States and Mexico, can separate, marginalize, and create conflict (Jamail 1981; Alvarez 1995). Together with a history of vigilantism and a criminal justice system which regularly countenances the use of force to maintain and encourage legal compliance, it seems hardly surprising that the United States, generally, and the border region, in particular, have witnessed the proliferation of civilian patrol groups "taking the law into their own hands".

7. Border Vigilantism

Just as vigilantism is not a new phenomenon in the United States, the MCDC is not the first time private citizens have taken it upon themselves to patrol the southern border of the United States. Many other civilian border patrol groups and efforts have existed, and continue to exist, that try to draw attention to the issue of undocumented immigration across the border (see Brooks 2005; Mansfield 2005; Baum 2006; Doty 2007; Walker 2007).[24] Despite the fact that the strategies and tactics used by these groups are manifold, the groups share a common goal and seem to have emerged for similar reasons. Walker (2007) has identified three main themes which appear to be widespread among contemporary civilian border patrol groups.

First and foremost, all of these groups seem to be motivated by a concern for national security. They argue that "the U.S. - Mexican border is relatively unprotected, with thousands of undocumented migrants crossing the border each month, and little or no actual barrier along most of the 2000-mile border" (Walker 2007: 151; see also Glon 2004; Doty 2007). Although attempts have been made to increase cooperation among the different administrative and protective agencies, to provide more federally authorized law enforcement officers, to implement newer and more advanced technology, or to use more far-reaching intelligence gathering devices, "these provisions are not enough to secure the Southern Border and prevent individuals of national security concern from entering the country" (Glon 2004: 351). For these groups, the reality of the situations is that "an illegal immigrant can literally drive a truck through the porous border at any time" (Glon 2004: 363); and they see the main cause for this situation in the federal government's failure to enforce existing immigration laws.

Secondly, these groups therefore put a strong emphasis on the rule of law. The rule of law is a concept which is embodied in the notion

---

[24] For example, in 1989/1990 some California residents formed a "Light Up the Border"-campaign, in which citizens illuminated a section of the border to prevent illegal border-crossing. *Friends of the Border Patrol* installed electronic surveillance at the border to assist with preventing undocumented migration and *No Invaders* utilizes the internet to promote its anti-immigrant movement by posting the contact information of suspected immigration law violators and those who help undocumented migrants (see Walker 2007; No Invaders 2008).

that the United States is a nation of laws and not of men. Under the rule of law, laws are thought to exist independent of, and separate from, human will. Border vigilantes consider enforcement to be critical to the integrity of the law (see Walker 2007). However, if the federal government does not adequately enforce immigration laws at the border, it is displaying "a careless disregard for one of the most fundamental principles of American society" (Gilchrist & Corsi 2006: 327). Thus, it is up to these border vigilantes to intervene in order to assist the state in protecting the border and in upholding the rule of law.

The last aspect which connects these various border groups is that they all demonstrate a "hint of xenophobia and/or nativism as motivating their actions" (Walker 2007: 152; see also Anthony 2005; Baum 2006; Rich 2006). Nativists are people who believe that America belongs to its native population and that the country's welfare is threatened by the presence of beliefs and actions of the foreign-born (see Gerstle 2004; Chacón & Davis 2007). Although these groups explicitly reject any characterization as nativist or even racist, their frequently expressed fear of a negative "foreign" influence on American culture or their belief in the incompatibility of the different cultures altogether, paints a different picture (see Huntington 2004; Gilchrist & Corsi 2006; Horwitz 2006; Rich 2006). While this "new" form of racism may be more subtle than the old "Jim Crow" racism, it remains racism nonetheless (Chacón & Davis 2007). In some cases, these groups even use openly racist stereotypes; for example, in criticizing immigration assimilation (see Huntington 2004).

To conclude, Part II has provided the theoretical background for this research. Vigilantism was defined and delineated from other forms of extra-legal violence based on Johnston's (1996) criminological definition. It was shown that vigilantism is a rather amorphous concept, which means that a specific occurrence of it can only be understood within its localized context. Therefore, the unique historical and legal context of American vigilantism, in particular, was presented. Lastly, the three ideological themes (national security, rule of law, xenophobia/nativism), which have been identified as being common among border vigilante groups, were identified. In the following part, these themes will be used to delineate the MCDC as a type of border vigilante.

PART III: ON THE EMERGENCE OF THE MCDC

We must prevail, we will prevail. We shall overcome the effort by many to identify this movement as irresponsible; we will be victorious in proving the sceptics wrong. Our efforts will change the course of history and ignite others to stand with courage to make a change. Many are waiting for the outcome and will themselves be motivated with a new sense of activism; we will be leaders who will make a difference, role models who will influence future generations. Are you with us, Americans? If yes, then "let's roll"!
~ SOP Minuteman Civil Defense Corps

[The people] are where the law comes from, you see. For they chose the delegates who made the Constitution that provided for the courts...And so when your ordinary citizen sees [the justice system fail] he must take justice back into his own hands where it was once at the beginning of all things. Call this primitive, if you will. But so far from being a *defiance* of the law, it is an *assertion* of it – the fundamental assertion of self-governing men, upon whom our whole social fabric is based.
~ Wister 1902: 435-36

The third part of this project introduces the MCDC and defines it as a form of border vigilantism. This is followed by an analysis of the way in which the MCDC has come to regard (and is itself participating in the construction of) the undocumented immigrant as a threat. The argument is made that the MCDC perceives undocumented immigration across the U.S. – Mexico border as a threat because U.S. immigration policies and prevention techniques have not only failed in preventing undocumented immigration across the border, but have succeeded in establishing the border as a place of danger and threat. In addition, media attention to undocumented immigration has not only increased steadily since the 1970s, but the media has also increasingly employed terms like "aliens," "flood," or "invasion" to describe these immigrants, which has served to further solidify this perception of the migrants as a threat. Based on the interview data, it is illustrated how these images of the "illegal immigrant" as a threat to national security are reflected in the discursive practices of the Minutemen today. It is also shown how the events of September 11, 2001, have led to the securitization of undocumented immigration as a national security priority and, thereby, have created a space of exception on the U.S. – Mexico border, which has energized and legitimized the activities of the MCDC.

Finally, a brief but critical look is taken at recent changes in the way security is produced and "guaranteed" by the state. Here, the argument is made that increasing privatization in the security sector has given rise to a feeling of government unwillingness or inability to effectively deal with the perceived threats. This feeling is exacerbated by globalization and its associated forces of political and economic liberalization. Since the government is no longer able to give its citizens the security "guarantees" they need, the vigilantes have emerged to temporarily "stand in" for the state in its absence.

8. Defining the Minuteman Civil Defense Corps

The MCDC was founded in the spring of 2004 by a man named Chris Simcox.

Previously, Simcox had run an organization called *Civil Homeland Defense*, which he had started in October 2001 after moving to Tombstone, AZ[25]. "Chris had travelled from California and had stopped at all the national parks and had seen what was coming across: the weapons and the drugs and the people," recalls the MCDC's Vice-President, "He knew he had to do something" (Author Interview #1: 90-93). Simcox started the *Civil Homeland Defense* organization and began to organize border observation patrols. He also bought the local newspaper, the *Tombstone Tumbleweed*, because "he knew it was going to be a privately owned newspaper and whatever he was going to write was going to come out and it wasn't going to be edited out as it is happening with so many media organizations" (Author Interview #1: 119-130). This way he had a platform from which he could raise awareness of the immigration "problem" at the southern border.

Almost two years later, in the fall of 2004, Simcox met Jim Gilchrist, a Marine Corps veteran and retired CPA, in Los Angeles where they were both giving on-air interviews on the topic of undocumented immigration (Gilchrist & Corsi 2006). In his book *Minutemen: The Battle to Secure America's Borders* (2006) Gilchrist writes that he was impressed by Simcox's passion and determination, and he approached Simcox to join efforts (see also Author Interviews #1 & #2). He was convinced that "by sending a few volunteers to the border, Simcox had created a springboard from which they could launch a movement against illegal immigration" (Gilchrist & Corsi 2006: 6). To him, Simcox was a "political pioneer" (Gilchrist & Corsi 2006: 6). That same fall, the *Minuteman Project* was created, and in October the *Minuteman Project* began its first big offensive.

Simcox and Gilchrist used the *Tombstone Tumbleweed* to put a call out for citizens to come to the Arizona-Mexico border in the spring of the following year so they could get together a volunteer "militia" that

---

[25] Tombstone, AZ, is also the site of the famous historical Wild West shootout at the OK Corral between Wyatt Earp's men and a gang of cowboys (see http://www.cityoftombstone.com/; last visited on26 September 2008).

would monitor and report undocumented immigrants. On April 1, 2005, "more than one thousand" volunteers gathered along Arizona's border with Mexico to patrol a stretch of 23 miles and stand watch (Author Interview #1: 14-20; see also Gilchrist & Corsi 2006: xix; Jordan 2005). The operation lasted thirty days and was claimed a huge success by the organizers. For one, the event had received tremendous coverage by the media (see Author Interview #1). In this regard, Simcox and Gilchrist had reached their goal of raising national awareness. Secondly, the Minutemen had stopped "essentially all illegal crossings following just ten days on the job" (Gilchrist & Corsi 2006: 8). The next twenty days they simply stood watch. For Simcox and Gilchrist "the question of whether or not America's porous borders could be guarded had been settled. The Minuteman Project had proven that all it required was the will to do so" (Gilchrist & Corsi 2006: 8).

Shortly thereafter, however, Simcox separated from the *Minuteman Project* and Gilchrist due to irreconcilable differences in "the way they wanted to do politics" (Author Interview #2: 11). Instead, he teamed up with the current Vice-President to start the MCDC – "one of the most important, socially responsible, and peaceful movements for justice since the civil rights movement of the 1960s."

8.1 Motivation

Based on the Minuteman Pledge and the Preface to their website, the Minutemen express three main concerns as motivating their actions.

The MCDC's first and foremost concern appears to be the protection of the United States "from invasion by enemies foreign and domestic" (see MCDC 2008). Although the Minutemen admit that "the human flood breaching our Homeland Defense is not necessarily the enemy per se; drug dealers, criminals, and potential terrorists are" (see MCDC 2008). Yet, seven years post September 11, 2001, they feel that the federal government still "is more concerned with securing the borders of foreign lands than securing the borders of the United States" and that "our borders are still wide open" (see MCDC 2008).

Moreover, the Minutemen feel that by not securing the nation's borders and enforcing immigration laws, the federal government is displaying a "blatant disregard" (see MCDC 2008) for the rule of law. This, they argue, has serious consequences for the nation's sovereignty.

Lastly, the Minutemen believe that if the "tidal wave" (see MCDC 2008) of people illegally entering into the United States isn't stopped, it will lead to a breakdown of the American infrastructure because undocumented immigrants get jobs at much lower wage and are "thus destroying the living wage, the people of the United States of America deserve" (see MCDC 2008).

In short, even though the government "owes the citizens of the United States protection from people who wish to take advantage of a free society," it is failing to "secure our borders, enforce our nation's sovereignty and end the flood of illegal trafficking into American territory" (see MCDC 2008). As a result, so the Minutemen, Americans face a "grave threat" to the security, sovereignty, and prosperity of their nation (see MCDC 2008).

8.2 Activities

Due to the federal government's shortcomings in protecting the interests of the Minutemen, the Minutemen regard it as their mission "to see the borders and coastal boundaries of the United States secured against the unlawful and unauthorized entry of all individuals, contraband, and foreign military" (see MCDC 2008). They want to challenge the government "to fulfil its constitutionally mandated responsibility [...] by fulfilling their obligation in their absence" (see MCDC 2008). This they hope to accomplish by using "every legal means at our disposal to assist law enforcement authorities in identifying and apprehending those who violate our borders," by "reporting to the proper authorities any business entity which knowingly recruits, facilitates or employs people who have entered America illegally," and by employing "all means of civil protest, demonstration, and political lobbying to accomplish this goal" (see MCDC 2008).

On a practical level, this means that the Minutemen go out on the border every weekend to observe, report, record and direct Border Patrol to suspected "illegal immigrants". They act as "the eyes and ears" of Border Patrol (Author Interview #1: 932). After calling the suspected "illegal immigrants" in, they wait for Border Patrol to come and apprehend them. For the legal reasons stated earlier in this work (see Chapter 4.2.3), the Minutemen are not allowed to detain any immigrants themselves; if they do so, they run a high risk of violating the law. Every April and October, the Minutemen organize two large thirty-day operations on the border, and they have begun building a fence. They also hold rallies in front of the labor sites where day laborers usually come to look for work. In addition, they are trying to get involved in the legislature not only on a local level by speaking at city council meetings or school board meetings, but also by lobbying directly in Washington D.C.

8.3 Organization

The MCDC is incorporated as a 501(c)(4) non-profit organization. According to the MCDC's Vice-President, the organization has about a hundred chapters in thirty-one states all across the country (see Author Interview #1). These chapters differ from state to state with regard to their activities. Border states, like Texas, Arizona or California, conduct border operations and work in local government. Non-border states concentrate on local government work only, which means that they attempt to affect laws or to enforce laws already in existence (see Author Interview #2).

The MCDC also has a political action committee (PAC), a search and rescue team and a foundation. Whereas the Minuteman PAC mainly seeks to influence policy and legislation, the search and rescue team goes out into the desert to try and "rescue bodies" (Author Interview #1: 406-10). The Minuteman Foundation's main responsibility is to educate (see Author Interview #1).

The MCDC does not have members. Aside from the board of directors, the organization almost entirely depends on volunteers (see Author Interview #2). The MCDC claims to have over ten thousand active volunteers and "probably several hundred thousand, several million" when they hold special operations (Author Interview #1: 1297-99). These volunteers supposedly come from all different backgrounds. They are said to include retired police officers, military or border patrol agents, as well as a lot of young people (see Author Interviews #1 & #2). The volunteers "really come from all walks of life" (Author Interview #1: 378). About 15% of the volunteers are female and 85% are male (see Author

Interview #2). Most importantly, however, they all share the "right" attitude:

> They're patriotic, they believe in the rule of law, they don't like what's happening on the border, they don't like what's happening to the middle class in America because of low wages from illegals and so that's what defines them (Author Interview #2: 268-71).

New volunteers are actively recruited at events like rodeos, fairs, gun shows, sportsmen shows or swap shops (see Author Interview #2). Anyone who is interested in participating in a border watch operation can also sign up on the MCDC's website. After agreeing to the terms of the Standard Operation Procedure, a registration fee must be paid which will put the applicant through a background check and a telephone interview. Once the applicant has completed the vetting process, he or she must also go through training and a briefing before he or she can go out on the border. This process serves to "weed people out who may be racist" because, as the MCDC's Vice-President says, "there's different characters, you know, and not everybody is always on the same think" (Author Interview #1: 299, 1404).

8.4 The MCDC as Border Vigilantes

When President Bush first called the Minutemen "vigilantes," the organizers of the MCDC were outraged. The Minutemen see themselves rather as "peace-loving and law abiding" citizen activists, who are seeking a peaceful resolution to the "chaotic neglect" at the border, than as vigilantes (see Author Interview #1). Nevertheless, the MCDC's State Director concedes that "the idea of the vigilante has a wonderful place in American lore" (Author Interview #2: 810). "They performed a function," he explains (Author Interview #2: 811-12). Then he adds, "Well, it looks just like out here. You don't see a sheriff's car around here, you don't see it. We have to take care of ourselves...out here." However, today, he says, the word "has a negative connotation" (Author Interview #2: 827), and although the Minutemen may be "old-fashioned vigilantes," they are "not new-fashioned vigilantes" (Author Interview #2: 829-30).

In deciding whether or not the MCDC can be classified as a vigilante organization, the criminological definition put forward by Johnston (1996), which was introduced in the second part of this work, can be helpful. Based on that definition, if the MCDC were a vigilante organization, it would have to be (a) composed of autonomous citizens who are (b) engaging in premeditated acts of force or threatened force. Those acts would (c) have to be focused on crime and/or social control and would (d) have to aim at offering security "guarantees" both to participants and to other members of a given established order. Lastly, the MCDC would have to have arisen as a reaction to the transgression of institutionalized norms by individuals or groups – or to their potential or imputed transgression.

8.4.1 Voluntary Activity Engaged in by Autonomous Citizens

As was noted above, the MCDC is a group of private citizens who are voluntarily engaging in border patrolling activity. Although it might be argued that the MCDC fails to satisfy the "autonomous" citizenship requirement because it is incorporated, this contention should be rejected for the following reasons.

First, the fact that the Minutemen are only allowed to patrol on private ranch land indicates that they hold no special permission or authorization granted by the federal government. Secondly, the MCDC is incorporated as a non-profit organization, which means that it is also not engaging in commercial enterprise. More importantly, however, nothing in the relationship between the MCDC and the federal government or Border Patrol, stipulates that the MCDC receives either direct or indirect financial, political, or other support from them.

To the contrary, when the MCDC first emerged, the government wanted to "get rid" of them and "shut [the Minutemen] down" (Author Interview #1: 198, 757). Even applying for the 501(c)(4) status took a long time because "the government didn't want us to have it" (Author Interview #1: 1120). In the process, the MCDC was checked out by both the FBI and the CIA to make sure it was operating within the legal confines. The Minutemen were told that the way they operated, there was nothing wrong with them. As long as they kept operating that way, the government said it "wouldn't be able to do anything about them" (Author Interview #1: 760-765).

The Minutemen's relationship with the U.S. Border Patrol seems no different. They, too, kept their distance at first because they thought the Minutemen were "vigilantes". "We were carrying guns and we were in the desert and we had our flashlights and so...they were very weary at first and they were watching us," says the Vice-President (Author Interview #1: 922-25). Even though their relationship allegedly got better over time and evolved into one of "mutual respect" (Author Interview #1: 941), to this day Border Patrol is

> not supposed to really do much with us formally. So at the very top they wouldn't talk to us...at the very top I think that would be bad for their career if they were seen ehm talking to the Minutemen and cooperating with the Minutemen (Author Interview #2: 197-202).

Clearly, the relationship between the Minutemen and the Border Patrol might be one of "mutual respect," but it is not one of "mutual support". Therefore, the MCDC fulfils the "autonomous" citizenship requirement.

8.4.2 Premeditated Acts of Force or Threatened Force

In Arizona, no state permit is required to purchase or possess a shotgun, rifle or handgun.[26] For this reason, most MCDC volunteers in Arizona carry firearms. Going out into the desert without a handgun or a sidearm, says the MCDC's State Director, "is a situation that is sufficiently dangerous that, even though we're not gun-central, it's nice to have a handgun - just in that long shot that something would go awry" (Author Interview #2: 134-136). Since the borderlands are an area where "there's more violence than meets the eye" (Author Interview #2: 718) and where a "component of violence" is "always there even when you seem to be looking at the most innocent of people" (Author Interview #2: 726-27), something could go awry very quickly. Yet, as the State Director points out,

---

[26] The only restrictions apply to so-called "prohibited possessors" (Ariz. Rev. Stat. Ann. §13-3101 (A) (6)). Arizona is an "open-carry" state, which means that the firearm must be immediately accessible and carried openly in a way that makes it obvious to a casual observer the person is carrying a deadly weapon.

> [t]he Minutemen get very seldomly involved anyway in that. We just don't have any – because there's no need to. It doesn't – it wouldn't benefit us. And eh it wouldn't help to do our job (Author Interview #2: 727-730).

And he adds:

> We try to be very careful. I'm sure cranks could slip through the system as they do in any large group but they don't last. They get caught and they get thrown out (Author Interview #2: 290-92).

Even if they didn't get caught, "[i]t would be impossible to get away with it on the border, Border Patrol are all over the place and nearby, they'd have to report it" (Author Interview #2: 761-62). But "getting away with it is not the issue. We just don't do it," so the State Director (Author Interview #2: 762-763), and the Vice-President agrees: "We have *never* had anybody fired at...[and] we have never had anybody pull their weapon from their holster" (Author Interview #2: 112-14).

At this point, any definition of vigilantism as "extra-legal violence" would deny that the MCDC classifies as a vigilante organization. Johnston's definition, however, neither assumes vigilante activity to be extra-legal nor to involve the actual use of force. It suffices that the use of force is threatened, and this is certainly the case with the MCDC.

As mentioned previously, although the MCDC explicitly distances itself from any use of violence, almost all of the Minutemen carry at least a sidearm. They are also willing to use their sidearm, if need be, not only to protect themselves out in the desert, but also to enforce their message. "If the federal government doesn't come back and respond to the people, we will be [ready to take up arms]," explains the MCDC's Chapter Director (Author Interview #3: 377).

What is more, the MCDC certainly has all the trappings of a military campaign. Aside from carrying guns, the Minutemen arrive at their border watches equipped with military fatigues, binoculars, bulletproof vests and walkie-talkies. This makes sitting out on the border during a watch feel almost like being in a warzone; and many of the Minutemen volunteers are indeed former military or law enforcement officers (see Author Interview #1; see also Walker 2007; Doty 2007; Chacón & Davis

2007). Finally, the use of military terminology in communication between the volunteers undoubtedly also contributes to this atmosphere of immanent violence.

Likewise, there is no doubt that the activities of the MCDC are premeditated. From the first recruitment of volunteers and the organization of border watches, to the standard operating procedure that lays down exactly how to conduct the operations, everything appears well thought-out and planned. The second requirement of Johnston's definition is fulfilled.

8.4.3 Focus on Crime and/or Social Control

Thirdly, in order to classify as vigilantism, the activities of the Minutemen would have to be focused on crime and/or social control.

Ostensibly, it is the MCDC's mission to secure the southern border of the United States and to prevent the "unlawful and unauthorized entry of all individuals, contraband, and foreign military" (MCDC 2008) across it. In this effort, the MCDC not only tries to physically seal off the border by conducting border operations, it also tries to attempt new immigration laws and to push for the enforcement of immigration laws that are already in existence. By engaging in these efforts, the Minutemen claim to have contributed to the defeat of several amnesty bills by now (see Author Interview #1). They are avid proponents of the *E-Verify* system (see Author Interviews #1 and #3), an online system which allows employers to check the work status of potential employees, and are now pushing to have the Senate pass the *SAFE Act*, an amendment to the *USA Patriot Act*. In addition, the MCDC's Chapter Director has been actively involved in passing the *Legal Arizona Workers Act* (LAW), which was signed into law in 2007 and went into effect January 1st, 2008. Under this law, all employers are required to use the *E-Verify* system to check a potential employee's work status. Employers who "knowingly" or "intentionally" hire illegal workers risk having their business license temporarily suspended. If they are caught a second time, their business license will be revoked.

From the point of view of the Minutemen, therefore, it might surely be said that all of these efforts seek to put an end to, or at least control, the crime of unauthorized entry into the United States.

However, while on the one hand the Minutemen say they seek to uncover unfair and exploitative employment practices (what they call the "new slave trade" or "21st century slavery" (see Author Interview #3)), they are at the same time attacking the labor unions' rights to organize migrants (Chacón & Davis 2007). They claim that unions, like the *American Civil Liberties Union* (ACLU) or the *United Farm Workers* (UFW), are actively aiding and abetting "aliens" attempting to enter the country illegally (Chacón & Davis 2007). In doing so, the Minutemen are actually contributing to the increased criminalization of immigrants. What is more, through their activities and rhetoric they are not only reinforcing a defensive stance toward immigration among the public, but are further solidifying perceptions of labor migrants as "illegal".

Hence, the main focus of the MCDC may not be the control of crime after all, but rather the protection of their middle-class privileges as American citizens (see also Chacón & Davis 2007). Either way, the third element in Johnston's definition of vigilantism is present.

8.4.4 Aim to Offer Security "Guarantees"

Lastly, the Minutemen's activities would have to aim at offering security "guarantees" both to participants and to other members of the established order. This means that their activities would have to be motivated by the desire "to do something" to minimize threat to persons, property, or values and to reduce associated fear (see Johnston 1996).

The biggest focus of the MCDC, for its Vice-President, is "getting that border secured for national security and public safety" (Author Interview #1: 314-15). As was already shown above, in order to do that, the MCDC not only tries to cooperate with Border Patrol and to physically seal off the border by conducting border operations, it also tries to attempt new immigration laws and to push for the enforcement of immigration laws that are already in existence. In addition, the MCDC claims to be concerned about the personal security of those citizens living in the border region who directly experience the undocumented immigrants coming across the border (see Author Interviews #1, #2 and #3). They say that they have been asked by several ranchers to patrol their lands and help protect them, their families and their property against the influx of "illegal immigrants":

> And when we met the ranchers, they called us one day and ehm I mean, there are so many trails on this ranch [.] that the illegals have literally stomped with their feet. Sometimes they are this wide (She spreads her arms apart to demonstrate the width of the trail.). That many. And there's hundreds of'em - hundreds of'em. And so when we came here and the rancher took us out and well we said: "This is where we're going to set up." And they wanted us here, they were happy, you know, that we came. They couldn't even go out to town. Their little granddaughter couldn't even play outside anymore. Because they were hiding everywhere. They were hiding in their barns, you know. Many many times the little girl [..] got into contact with some of the illegals. And it was scary, you know (Author Interview #1: 792-802).

Due to their presence and their activities, the MCDC's Vice-President says, the Minutemen were able to reduce the rancher's fear for his family and his home:

> So, now that we're here there's usually somebody always staying around and the rancher can go. They can even take a little vacation because they know we're going to watch the ranch for them, you know (Author Interview #1: 802-805).

The Minutemen also aim to offer assurances of peace to citizens who are concerned about the influx of immigrants by educating them and informing them about the situation at the border, the impact of immigration on the United States, or even the infectious diseases that immigrants can bring into the country (see Author Interview #1 and #2). In a way, they even give assurance to people by inviting them to see with their own eyes what is going on at the border (see Author Interview #1). It can be argued that this, in the very least, heightens the people's sense of security by giving them the feeling that they themselves are "doing something" about their own security.

To conclude, the Minutemen are clearly demonstrating a concern for minimizing threat to persons, property, or values and for reducing associated fear. The last requirement of Johnston's definition of vigilantism has equally been fulfilled.

Thus, based on Johnston's criminological definition of vigilantism, it can safely be concluded that the MCDC does classify as a vigilante organization, and, for the remainder of this text, it will be treated as such. After having defined the MCDC as a type of border vigilante organization, the next sections now turn to the emergence of the MCDC. In these sections, a closer look is taken at the history of U.S. immigration policies and prevention strategies with a view to understanding how the MCDC has come to regard the ("illegal") immigrant as a national security threat.

9. Immigration Control and the Rise of the "Criminal Alien"

Ever since the establishment of the U.S. – Mexico border through the *Treaty of Guadalupe Hidalgo* in 1848, immigration across the southern border has been one of the most important issues between the United States and Mexico. Yet, for almost another fifty years after its establishment, the southern border of the United States remained relatively uncontrolled, and Mexicans were able to traverse the border without any great difficulty. At that time "illegal" immigration was, therefore, virtually impossible.

9.1 1875-1940: Creation of the "Illegal Immigrant"

The first time that "undesirable" immigrants were officially denied entry into the United States was in 1875. In that year, Congress passed the so-called *Page Act* which barred prostitutes and criminals from entering the United States (Tichenor 2002; Ngai 2003; U.S. CIS 2008; see also Appendix 1). The first general immigration law was not passed until seven years later, in 1882. Written during "a fit of anti-Asian sentiment" (Ellingwood 2004: 20), this law mainly applied to Chinese and Japanese immigrants who were arriving in the United States by vessel. Although one consequence of it was that authorities paid more attention to the nation's border with Canada and to its seaports (U.S. CIS 2008), a focus on Mexican immigration and the "porous" Mexican border did not emerge until later.

What did already emerge at that time, however, were a growing anti-immigrant sentiment and a surge in political nativism, which Tichenor (2002) and Ngai (2003) attribute to the dramatic increases in the volume and ethnic diversity of immigration to the United States during the 1850s. Especially in the final decade of the 19th century, Tichenor (2002) writes, new immigrants became increasingly linked to alleged increases in crime, poverty, and public expenditures on poor relief and law enforcement. Or, as in the case of the 1886 bombing of Haymarket Square in Chicago[27], even with terrorism, labor upheaval, and political radicalism

---

[27] During a nation-wide strike for the 8-hour workday, which was initiated by the *Knights of Labor*, a mass meeting was held in the Chicago haymarket to protest a police action of the previous day in which workers were killed. When police

(Tichenor 2002). These sentiments only waned slightly when, after the turn of the century, industrialization took hold of the United States and, as a result, immigration and the creation of a cheap labor base for American agriculture and industry temporarily became a necessity to meet the demands of this new market (see Ngai 2003; Portes & Rumbaut 2006; Walker 2007). It was at this time that major Mexican immigration to the United States commenced. From the very beginning, the United States' stance toward it was an ambiguous one at best.

On the one hand, American employers were happy to have Mexican workers come to the United States because they were needed to fill the labor shortages created by the rapid industrialization and expansion of the agricultural, manufacturing and mining sectors (see Tichenor 2002; Glon 2004; Ellingwood 2004). In addition, out of all the non-Anglo-Saxon groups entering the United States at that time, Mexicans were still considered the most "inconspicuous" (Reisler 1976: 232). On the other hand, the Mexican immigrant was also regarded "less desirable as a citizen than as a laborer" (Reisler 1976: 232), and while Mexicans undoubtedly were "durable" and "uncomplaining" workers (Reisler 1976: 232), the government hoped that only very few of them would eventually decide to become citizens of the United States (see also Ellingwood 2004). In fact, according to a 1911 report by the Dillingham Commission on immigration, the government considered this to be very likely because of the Mexican's "strong attachment to [his] native land...and the possibility of their residence here being discontinued" (quoted in Ellingwood 2004: 20).

By the 1920s, the system of mass industrial production had matured to a point where increased output no longer resulted from continuously increasing input of unskilled labor, but from technological improvement (Ngai 2003; see also Portes & Rumbaut 2006; Chacón & Davis 2007). With this development, the need for immigrant laborers quickly declined and the federal government expected most of the Mexi-

---

ordered the protest meeting to disperse, a bomb was thrown. According to Tichenor (2002), in the aftermath, the bombing was hastily attributed to seven anarchists of whom six were immigrants. This persuaded many Americans that terrorism, labor upheaval, and political radicalism originated abroad because, as an American journal insisted at that time, "there is no such thing as an American anarchist. [...] The American character has in it no element which can under any circumstances be won to uses so mistaken" (quoted in Tichenor 2002:71).

can workers to return to their homeland. Instead, immigration rates continued to climb.

In subsequent years, this led to the passage of several laws which attempted to regulate and restrict immigration to the United States; the most notable of these laws being the Immigration Acts of 1921 and 1924. Both of these Acts imposed limitations on the number of immigrants of any nationality that could legally enter the United States (U.S. CIS 2008).[28] However, while these quota laws effectively reduced the number of legal immigrants, they also had an unintended side effect, they "stimulated the production of illegal aliens" (Ngai 2003: 70).

In 1924, Congress therefore for the first time also enacted a law which provided for a serious enforcement mechanism against unlawful entry: a land Border Patrol (Tichenor 2002; Ngai 2003; U.S. CBP-Hist. 2008). Up until this point in time, the nation's borders had remained, for the most part, unguarded (Andreas 2003; Ellingwood 2004; U.S. CBP-Hist. 2008). Although inspection at arrival sought to identify excludable persons and deny them admission, little could be done, if the immigrants avoided the inspection stations and instead entered the United States at different points in between (Ngai 2003). From now on, this would be different. Additionally, the Act of 1924 established a "consular control system" which required all prospective immigrants to the United States to obtain a visa from a consular official of the U.S. Department of State in their own homeland prior to admittance (U.S. CIS 2008). For many Mexican laborers this requirement was a significant burden and, thus, was often ignored (Glon 2004). Instead, most Mexican immigrants continued to cross the border informally, but "what had once been legal, was now considered illegal by the U.S. government" (Glon 2004: 354). Mexican immigrants who were already in the country but had failed to obtain a visa prior to entry were deported and warned not to return (see Glon 2004; U.S. CIS 2008).

---

[28] The Immigration Act of 1921 set the national limit for legal immigration to the United States at 350,000 annually. Two years later, Congress further restricted immigration to 150,000 per year. Quotas were allocated to countries in proportion to the numbers that the American people traced their "national origin" to those countries (see Ngai 2003; U.S.CIS Immigration Legislation Summary 2008).

The overall result of these first legislative efforts, therefore, was the creation of a new class of persons within the national body: "illegal immigrants". What is more, the increase in the number of illegal entries created an emphasis on control of the nation's contiguous land borders that had not existed before (Ellingwood 2004; Rodriguez 2006; Eigmüller/Vobruba 2006). "This new articulation of state territoriality reconstructed national borders and national space in ways that were both highly visible and problematic," writes Ngai (2003: 71). What resulted from this new articulation was an oppositional political and legal discourse, which imagined "deserving" and "undeserving" or "desirable" and "undesirable" immigrants and, concomitantly, just and unjust deportations (Ngai 2003; see also Vukov 2003). It also led to the emergence of the Mexican immigrant as the iconic "illegal alien".[29]

Finally, the creation of the "illegal alien" also contributed to the fact that the mere idea of persons without formal legal status residing in the nation came to be connected to images of great danger (Ngai 2003). This is exemplified by a report of the Immigration and Naturalization Service (INS), which as early as 1925, warned that

> [i]t is quite possible that there is an even greater number of aliens in the country whose legal presence here could not be established. No estimate could be made as to the number of smuggled aliens who have been unlawfully introduced into the country since the quota restrictions of 1921...The figures presented are worthy of serious thought, especially when it is considered that there is such a great percentage of our population...whose first act upon reaching our shores was to break our

---

[29] Whereas Canadian and especially European immigrants tended to be associated with a romanticized image of the "noble" immigrant arriving at Ellis Island, and disassociated from the real and imagined category of the "illegal immigrant" (something which facilitated their national and racial assimilation as white Americans), this positive national perception of immigrants did not transfer when migrants began arriving across America's southern border (see Walker 2007; Tichenor 2002; Ngai 2003; Rodriguez 2006). To the contrary, illegal status became "constitutive of a racialized Mexican identity and of the Mexican's exclusion from the national community and polity" (Ngai 2003: 72; see also Rodriguez 2006).

laws by entering in a clandestine manner – all of which serves to emphasize the potential source of trouble, not to say menace, that such a situation suggests (INS Annual Report 1925: 12-13).

In that same year, an estimated 1.4 million undocumented immigrants were already thought to be living in the United States (see Ngai 2003). The INS was alarmed and the federal government soon responded by placing additional restrictions on immigration.

In the spring of 1929, undocumented immigrants were criminalized for good, after Congress passed a law which made unlawful entry a misdemeanor and a second unlawful entry a felony punishable by imprisonment and/or a fine (U.S. CIS 2008). Also, the federal government had begun deporting immigrants of Mexican descent on a large scale, including many legal residents and American citizens because they held them partially responsible for high unemployment rates during the economic crisis (Rodriguez 2006; Walker 2007). Almost half of the Mexican population in the United States was deported during that time, often even at considerable expense. However, despite these ever more restrictive immigration policies, immigration from Mexico continued to increase (Glon 2004).

9.2 1940-1980: Rise of the "Criminal Alien"

In 1942, the United States entered World War II and, as was the case during the First World War, this created a new demand for cheap labor to work on farmlands and in factories (see Glon 2004; Ellingwood 2004). Again, migrant workers from Mexico were welcomed into America to fill labor shortages throughout the country (see Glon 2004; Rodriguez 2006; Walker 2007; Chacón & Davis 2007). It was at this time, that Congress passed a number of laws allowing for the legal importation of temporary Mexican workers.

9.2.1 The Bracero-Program

The most well-known of these laws is probably the Act of April 29th, 1943, which provided for the importation of temporary agricultural laborers to the United States (U.S. CIS 2008). This Act served as the legal framework for the Mexican *Bracero*-Program. The *Bracero*-Program was an agreement between the governments of the United States and Mexico that gave Mexicans permission to cross the border for temporary jobs as laborers or so-called *braceros*[30].

Although the *Bracero*-Program did bolster agricultural prosperity during and after the war, by the time the program actually ended in 1964, it was heavily criticized. In the almost 22 years that the program was in effect, over 4.8 million Mexican workers had been legally hired to work in the United States (see Durand et al. 1995; Tichenor 2002; Rodriguez 2006; Walker 2007). Earning less than minimum wage, many American employers were happy to have them. One grower reportedly said, "We used to own slaves, now we rent them from the government" (quoted in Ellingwood 2004: 22). Still, the number was much higher than the program had provided for. In addition, the program had given rise to a nationwide concern about employer abuses and exploitation (Ellingwood 2004; Bacon 2007; Chacón & Davis 2007). The most fervently criticized point, however, was that many of these workers did not return to Mexico after the program ended. "Once they worked in U.S. fields and on American railroads, many of the Mexican workers were hooked," writes Ken Ellingwood (2004: 22). Even if the wages were cut-rate by American standards, they represented more than workers could make in Mexico (Ellingwood 2004). Once the workers decided to stay in the United States though, they were instantly transformed from legal to illegal status.

In the end, the *Bracero*-Program resulted not only in a rise of legal and illegal immigration, but also served to finally construct the Mexican as a migratory agricultural laborer (Tichenor 2002; Ngai 2003; Glon 2004). Combined with the perception of the Mexican as the iconic "illegal alien," this gave powerful sway to the notion that Mexicans had no rightful presence on United States territory.

9.2.2 Operation Wetback

About midway into the *Bracero*-Program, the increases in undocumented immigration were so dramatic that they heightened pressure on national policymakers to respond (Tichenor 2002). While in 1949 over 280,000 illegal immigrants were seized by the United States Border Patrol, by

---

[30] The word *bracero* is rooted in *brazo*, the Spanish word for "arm".

1953, the number of those seized had grown to over 860,000 (Glon 2004). Newspaper articles as well as radio stories abounded with sensational accounts of the public health risks, criminal activity, exploitation, welfare dependency, and native job displacement that accompanied large-scale undocumented immigration (Tichenor 2002; Chavez 2008).

Feeling pressure to address this "flood" of "illegal immigration" and the growing public concern, Congress passed the *Wetback Act*[31] in 1952. This Act allowed Border Patrol agents to enter both public and private lands in order to seek out and detain undocumented immigrants (see Inda 2006; Walters 2008; U.S. CIS 2008). It also criminally sanctioned anyone who smuggled or harboured immigrants that had not been inspected and legally admitted (U.S. CIS 2008). Two years later, the INS launched *Operation Wetback,* which became the "first large-scale, systematic implementation of military strategy and tactics by the INS against Mexican immigrants" (Walker 2007: 143; see also Tichenor 2002; Inda 2006; Walters 2008). Its goal was not only to capture "illegal aliens" and to deport them en masse, but to put an end to undocumented immigration altogether (Rodriguez 2006; Walters 2008). In the following months, a wave of dragnet raids swept across the Southwest, and thousands of Mexican immigrants were rounded up as part of this Operation (Tichenor 1994; Inda 2006; Walters 2008). In 1954 alone, over one million Mexican nationals were arrested and over 300,000 deported (see Tichenor 2002; Ellingwood 2004; Rich 2006; U.S. CBP-Hist. 2008). Then Attorney General Herbert Brownell justified the "drive against illegal Mexican labor" as necessary "to wipe out the disease, criminal activity, juvenile delinquency, and social instability that attends any wetback invasion" (quoted in Tichenor 2002: 202). And indeed, the number of annual apprehensions of undocumented immigrants along the U.S. – Mexican border decreased in subsequent years (see Tichenor 2002; Ellingwood 2004).[32]

---

[31] The term *wetback* is a derogatory term for a person who has come into the United States illegally. It is commonly referring to Mexicans. The term originated with those undocumented immigrants who entered Texas by crossing the Rio Grande, presumably by swimming or wading across and getting his or her back wet in the process (see Ellingwood 2004).

[32] The number of apprehensions being made by the U.S. Border Patrol along the Southwest border is the most commonly used indicator to measure effectiveness (see Cornelius 2001). In 1994, Espenshade (1994) found that, the typical undocumented immigrant, who is already in the country, faces an annual probabil-

As a result, in the years after the Eisenhower administration initiated *Operation Wetback*, the issue of undocumented immigration virtually disappeared from the public agenda and INS leadership confidently told Congress that the "problem of illegal immigration" had been resolved (Tichenor 2002; see also Ellingwood 2004). Still, beyond the media glare, INS agents allowed many arrested *wetbacks* to remain in the country as legal *bracero* workers (Tichenor 2002). Although the American Federation of Labor (AFL) protested that distinctions between undocumented immigrants and *braceros* were tenuous at best, they were largely ignored (Tichenor 2002). This practice led to a sharp increase in annual *bracero* admissions, which "more than doubled despite widespread employer violations of wage, hour, safety, and recruitment regulations" (Tichenor 2002: 202). In a way, in those years the United States shifted "from a de jure policy of active labor recruitment to a de facto policy of passive labor acceptance" (Durand et al. 1999: 519).

Almost simultaneously, the U.S. Border Patrol changed its official rhetoric with regard to undocumented immigration. When it previously spoke of "undesirable" immigrants or "immigrant aliens," it now preferred to use the words "criminal alien" whenever a criminal record existed, and, when no criminal record existed, the words "deportable alien" (Hernández 2006). Soon, even the term "deportable alien" was no longer deemed strong enough and it was substituted with the term "border violator". These changes were thought to have a profound psychological effect on the public and the courts that, so it was hoped, would eventually benefit the Service (Hernández 2006). They also marked the beginnings of a rhetoric which brought the increasing criminalization of the Mexican immigrant to a new level. The Mexican immigrant was no longer spoken of as a temporary, legal or illegal, docile laborer but as a "border violator" and criminal.[33]

---

ity of being apprehended of 1-2%. Despite the risk of apprehension at the border being about 30%, all migrants who make it to the border eventually make it into the country, because they keep coming back and keep trying until they are successful.

[33] In her article, Kelly Hernández, however, also argues that while it is true that the U. S. Border Patrol was the primary police force involved in migration control along the U. S.-Mexico border, "Mexican officials actively participated in the imagination and implementation of policing unsanctioned migration along the U. S.-Mexico border" (2006: 428). Although the interests of the United

One year after the end of the *Bracero*-Program, former U.S. President Lyndon Johnson signed the Immigration Act of 1965, which "drastically changed America's immigration law" (Glon 2004: 355). Most importantly, the Act reduced institutionalized racial discrimination by abolishing the national origins quota system (U.S. CIS 2008). But, according to Justin C. Glon, it also had the effect of "converting immigration admissions into a social and political policy that served the private interests of U.S. legal permanent residents and their relatives" (2004: 355). In addition, the limitations imposed on immigrants admitted from countries in the Western hemisphere created long waiting periods for Mexicans (over 2 ½ years) to immigrate legally (US. CIS 2008; Tichenor 2002). This, once again, caused a dramatic increase in undocumented immigration across the U.S. – Mexico border (see Ellingwood 2004; Glon 2004).

9.3 1980-2000: "Alien Invasion"

By the 1980s, the United States had become "overwhelmed" by the massive influx of "illegal immigrants" (Church 1984). "Estimates of how many illegal aliens are already in the U.S. run as high as 15 million; the Census Bureau's guess is somewhere between 3.5 million and 6 million. But there is no question that the tide is rising," ominously reported an article in TIME magazine (Church 1984). "[T]he steady stream of illegal immigrants is turning into a flood," warned another (Dowd 1983). And former U.S. President Ronald Reagan concluded, "We have lost control of our own borders, and no nation can do that and survive" (quoted in Church 1984). This "crisis" highlighted the extent to which national borders had become "porous" and "inadequately regulated" (Tichenor 1994: 333; see also Church 1984). It also meant that "[i]llegal immigration had now become a major problem in the United States and was gaining the attention of key politicians in Washington" (Glon 2004: 357). Two major laws shaped American immigration policy landscape in the 1980s and

---

States certainly dominated in U. S.-Mexican relations, she writes, Mexican officials participated in migration control along its northern border according to Mexico's domestic interests in regulating the international mobility of Mexican laborers (see Hernández 2006).

1990s: the *Immigration Reform and Control Act of 1986* (IRCA) and the Immigration Act of 1990.

The primary purpose of the IRCA was to remove "illegal immigrants" from the U.S. labor market (Chiswick 1988; see also Portes & Rumbaut 2006). It was hoped that by "wiping the slate clean" (Chiswick 1988: 114), the United States could start over and, once and for all, close the door to undocumented immigration. The way this goal was to be achieved was, on the one hand, by granting legal status or "amnesty" for certain undocumented immigrants, and on the other hand, by imposing penalties against employers who "knowingly" hire undocumented immigrants (U.S. CIS 2008; Ellingwood 2004; Tichenor 1994; Tichenor 2002; Glon 2004). These employer sanctions were intended to reduce the demands for cheap undocumented immigrant labor (Chiswick 1988). The legislation also created a seven-year agricultural worker program that expedited the availability of immigrant laborers and provided statutory protections for both American and foreign workers (U.S. CIS 2008; Glon 2004; Tichenor 2002).

Mexican immigrants were the largest group to apply for amnesty under provisions of the IRCA and more than two million of them were ultimately given legal status (see Tichenor 2002; Glon 2004; Ellingwood 2004). However, the legalization program was soon enough criticized as being counterproductive. The prospect of employment and amnesty, it was argued, only encouraged even more Mexicans to follow suit and enter the United States "illegally" (see Baker 1997; Glon 2004). In the long run, it also caused many more Mexicans to naturalize than ever before, because this was one way for them to remain in the country and protect themselves, their rights, privileges and interests (Durand et al. 1999). In addition, undocumented immigrants were often able to produce fake passports or other documents that would allow them to avoid apprehension and governmental sanction (Glon 2004). With legal papers in hand, they were free to travel and settle anywhere in the United States in search of better opportunities. Ultimately, the IRCA and its system of legalizations and employer sanctions failed to effectively curb undocumented immigration. After 1986, it flowed unabatedly (see Tichenor 2002; Glon 2004; Huntington 2004).

Of the Immigration Act of 1990 only two provisions specifically applied to undocumented immigration. The first provision once more revised the grounds for exclusion and deportation of undocumented immigrants, and the other increased the size of the Border Patrol (see U.S.CIS 2008; Glon 2004). The Act mainly had a big impact because it called for the implementation of a diversity program that encouraged immigration from countries that had demonstrated low levels of immigration to the United States since the 1965 Act.

9.3.1 Operation Gatekeeper

Only a couple of years later, when former U.S. President Bill Clinton took office in 1992, public frustration over "illegal immigration" had reached an all time high (Glon 2004). After all these years trying in vain to curb or at least control undocumented immigration, resentment was growing among the American public (Ellingwood 2004). The decades-long rhetoric of associating Mexican immigration with narratives of threat, danger, invasion and destruction of the American culture, was beginning to show its effects (see Chavez 2008). As a result, popular support for restricting immigration once again seemed to intensify across the country (see Nelan 1993; Gwynne 1994; Tichenor 2002).

The United States was also still waging the "War on Drugs" that former U.S. President George H.W. Bush had declared in 1989. Since its declaration, the antidrug campaign had quickly replaced anticommunism as the driving force of America's security policy in the border region (see Andreas 2003). As the "drug war" escalated in the early 1990s, many Latin American drug-exporting and transit countries deployed their militaries to the front lines at the border (see Tichenor 2002; Andreas 2003).

While previously the border's enforcement had been mainly a local issue, it now became a national concern. "Politicians and polemicists soon showed up [at the border] with cameras in tow to fulminate against a border in disarray – and, by extension, to warn of a nation under attack," writes Ellingwood (2004: 28). Standing right beside the fence that separates the United States from Mexico, Pat Buchanan allegedly turned to reporters and angrily told them that "the government was failing to protect its own borders from an 'illegal invasion' of at least a million people a year" (quoted in Ellingwood 2004: 28). Not surprisingly, this framing of the U.S. - Mexico border as something that is "lost" and across which "invaders" come soon coincided with calls to further militarize the border. And, although this rhetoric did not cause the militarization of the border, it "surely contributed to an atmosphere that helped to justify increased militarization of the border as a way of 'doing something' about these threats to the nation's security and the American way of life" (Chavez 2008: 34).

President Clinton and the United States Congress first viewed the North American Free Trade Agreement (NAFTA) as a possible solution to this dilemma (see Tichenor 1994). The idea was that NAFTA "would improve the economic situation in Mexico, and thus encourage would-be Mexican immigrants to stay within their homeland where work would now be available" (Glon 2004: 358; see also Espenshade 1995). In the end, NAFTA did improve the Mexican economy, but failed to solve the problem of undocumented immigration since most of the improvements were not being realized in the border regions (Tichenor 2002; see also Glon 2004; Ellingwood 2004). In the aftermath,

> [i]mmigrants came to be blamed for everything from the high cost of welfare to the fiscal crisis of the social service system. United States politicians deliberately encouraged the belief that the United States schools, hospitals, and public services were spending massive resources on immigrants, both legal and illegal, who came to the United States to take unfair advantage of public generosity and the taxes paid by ordinary United States citizens (Durand et al. 1999: 531).

To make matters worse, in late 1994, after a period of relatively high capital flows, the value of the Mexican national currency suddenly halved. As a consequence, the number of Mexicans living in extreme poverty approached almost 53%, as the neoliberal economic model demonstrated an inability to secure sufficient employment (Rosas 2006). This, of course, again primed immigration pressures.

At this point, rising alarm over the clandestine influx of people together with the "War on Drugs" almost naturally promoted "a fusion between United States national security and law enforcement missions" (Andreas 1996: 54). Hence, when NAFTA failed to produce the intended outcome, President Clinton's response was to implement a massive, almost military-style, offensive to seal the border (see Glon 2004; Ellingwood 2004).

This new border strategy was modelled on *Operation Hold the Line* which had been organized by the chief of Border Patrol Silvestre Reyes in El Paso, Texas, one year earlier (U.S. CBP-Hist. 2008). In an effort to prevent undocumented immigration through deterrence, Reyes had decided to station border patrol agents along the Rio Grande's concrete bank densely enough together to dissuade any crossers (see Cornelius 2001; Ellingwood 2004). The Operation was considered a "success" by the Border Patrol since the number of apprehensions plummeted almost immediately (U.S. CBP-Hist. 2008).

In 1994, *Operation Gatekeeper* was implemented and in that same year construction of a ten-foot wall along a fourteen-mile stretch of the California-Mexico border was begun (see Cornelius 2001; Ellingwood 2004). Because the nearly 2,000-mile border was too vast to seal all at once, the Operation focused on the most "troublesome" corridors, "pouring in agents as a general might concentrate troops and fortifying the zones with floodlights, fences, and an assortment of hardware, such as buried sensors, night-vision goggles and military-style infrared scopes" (Ellingwood 2004: 33-34). In the following years, the number of border patrol agents in California alone more than doubled from 980 in 1994 to 2,264 by June 1998, and the overall number of border patrol agents increased from 4,139 in 1992 to 7,982 in 1998 (Walker 2007). The U.S. military also assumed a variety of border policing duties (Andreas 2003). This was made possible by a partial loosening of the 1878 *Posse Comitatus Act*[34]. Even if not all of the undocumented immigrants coming across could be apprehended, it was reasoned that this "militarization" of the border would eventually deter any immigrant from even trying in the first place.

However, the political wave did not crest until 1996 with the passage of the *Illegal Immigration Reform and Immigration Responsibility Act* (IIRIRA) (see Durand et al. 1999; Tichenor 2002). The IIRIRA not only provided for stronger penalties against undocumented immigration, but also approved hiring of five thousand additional border patrol agents, increased punishment of those who smuggled illegal immigrants, and allowed for long-term detention of individuals who are awaiting a determination of their immigration status (see Glon 2004; U.S. CIS 2008;

---

[34] *Posse Comitatus* means "power of the county". It is Civil War-era law that prohibits military involvement in domestic law enforcement.

Meeropol 2006). Similar to the intentions behind *Operation Gatekeeper*, the Act was created to deter would-be "illegal immigrants" from even attempting to enter the United States (Espenshade 1995; Glon 2004). Over the next years, Border Patrol continued to grow in size and was apprehending greater numbers of undocumented immigrants each year (see U.S. CBP-Hist. 2008). Nonetheless, INS statistics also showed that the number of undocumented immigrants entering the United States without detection had increased at a rate of about 300,000 per year (see U.S. GOA 1997; Espenshade 1995; Glon 2004). Glon concludes that "it was obvious that NAFTA, the IIRIRA, and other immigration reforms had little success in slowing the tide of illegal immigrant to the United States" (2004: 360).

Although *Operation Gatek*eeper is said to have, at least temporarily, reduced illegal entries in San Diego by more than 75% and, like *Operation Hold the Line*, was considered a success by the U.S. Border Patrol, it also created a shift in migration across the border from California to Arizona and into less passable terrain (see U.S. CBP-Hist. 2008; Bersin 1996; Woodbury 1999; Ellingwood 2004; Walker 2007). This had several consequences for the immigrants. First, by moving illegal crossings to more remote areas in the desert or mountains, the number of immigrant fatalities increased.[35] In years past, undocumented immigrants coming across the border had "fallen prey to rapists and hardened killers, rain-engorged rivers, freeway traffic and their own ignorance and poor judgement" (Ellingwood 2004: 4), but now immigrants were dying each year because of dehydration, heat exhaustion, exposure or hypothermia (see Eschbach et al. 1999; Durand & Massey 1999; Cornelius 2001; Walker 2007). Between 1993 and 1997, Karl Eschbach et al. (1999) counted more than 1,600 possible migrant deaths at the southern border of the United States (see also Ruiz 2006).

Second, as traditional crossing points were shifting from urban, safer routes to rural, hazardous areas and more law enforcement was placed along the border, undocumented immigrants increasingly had to

---

[35] In March 2000, Amnesty International even passed a resolution stating that *Operation Gatekeeper* was an abuse of human rights because "it maximized the risk to migrants' lives – forcing them to cross the border either by swimming west around the fence or crossing further east in the hot and barren deserts of Arizona and New Mexico" (Walker 2007: 145).

rely on professional people-smugglers, so-called *coyotes* (see Andreas 1996; Eschbach et al. 1999; Walker 2007; Romero 2008). When immigrants perceive a higher chance of being apprehended while crossing the border, they are more likely to hire *coyotes,* found Pia Orrenius (2001) in a study that evaluated the IRCA and its effects on undocumented immigration. This in turn makes illegal entry more costly for the immigrants not only because the crossing is riskier, but also because the *coyotes* now have more clients.

For example, near Douglas, AZ, the typical charge to be smuggled across the border to Phoenix was $150 in 1999; by the summer of 2000, the fee had risen to anywhere between $800 - 1,300 per person (Cornelius 2001; see also Orrenia 2001); but these high fees neither guarantee that the immigrant reaches his or her destination safely and in good health, nor that he or she reaches the final destination at all. Many of the immigrants are exploited and abused, even before they reach the border (see Bersin 1996; Walker 2007). And finally, the more law enforcement tightens its control over the border, the more sophisticated these smuggling operations become. This eventually helps to create a monopoly for the particularly sophisticated smugglers and exposes the immigrants to even greater risk of exploitation and abuse (see Beare 1999; Cornelius 2001).

Operation Gatekeeper also had one big effect that is particularly relevant to this project. By sealing off the border in the California region and shifting immigration flows from there to Arizona, it drastically altered life for residents in many border towns (Ellingwood 2004). Describes Ellingwood:

> It didn't take long for that bulge [of illegal immigrants] to reach unsuspecting border communities, altering life dramatically for many denizens of America's borderlands. Tensions rose. Impoverished rural counties faced financial crises as they coped with the sudden expense of having to jail, hospitalize or bury the immigrants whose northward trips brought them to the countryside (2004: 5).

With the greater number of undocumented immigrants, the number of crimes against personal property increased (see DePalma 1995).

"The result of that [was] a very heightened sense of insecurity by residents...who in the past were not burdened with aliens and alien smugglers," writes DePalma (1995). "Those whose homes are near the line on the U.S. side must deal with constant incursions by strangers who may simply be looking for work -- but who may intend to rob, burglarize or something worse," explains Conover (1997) and he continues:

> [I]t's an area where until recently ranchers didn't really mind the kind of trespassing that took place -- small groups of Mexican workers who would close gates behind themselves and take only a drink of water as they passed through. But politics suddenly changed that. Operation Gatekeeper, a Clinton Administration initiative announced in 1994 to choke the high-visibility stream of aliens across the border near San Diego, has indeed been successful -- but mainly in moving the problem. Traffic is down near the city, but up 3,000 percent at places like the Border Patrol station at Campo, Calif., where arrests of illegal immigrants rose from 2,300 in 1994 to more than 78,000 in 1996.

As a result, the 1990s saw the emergence of the first civilian border patrols along the U.S. – Mexican border. The motivation of these groups echoed the decades-long discourse on Mexican immigration. Fed up by this "intrusion" and the "trails of trash left by hordes of immigrants trooping across their ranch lands" (Ellingwood 2004: 5), Arizona's ranchers were ready to take border enforcement into their own hands. Dressed in camouflage fatigues and carrying semiautomatic rifles,"[w]e get together at night and make a game out of it, who can catch the most," said one Arizona rancher interviewed by *New York Times* reporter Ted Conover (1997). Another rancher who actively seeks out undocumented immigrants trespassing on his land reportedly told a network news team: "Humans. That's the greatest prey there is on earth...They're your equal" (McGirk 2000). Roger Barnett, a former deputy sheriff turned rancher, has since been said to have inspired the foundation of many of the contemporary civilian border patrols (see McGirk 2000; Archibold 2006; Doty 2007). "The Barnetts, probably more than any people in this country, are responsible for the vigilante movement as it now exists," says Mark Potok, legal director of the *Southern Poverty Law Center* (SPLC), which tracks the groups. "They were the recipients of so much press coverage and they kept boasting, and it was out of those boasts that the modern vigilante movement sprang up" (quoted in Archibold 2006).

10. The MCDC, Illegal Immigration and National Security

The issue of immigration control and border security had already emerged as an increasingly salient topic in political discourse in the 1980s and 1990s. This trend, however, received additional impetus after the attacks on the World Trade Center on September 11, 2001. On the one hand, these attacks caused "the greatest-ever loss of American life by foreign actors on American soil" (Walker 2007: 146), on the other, they "jolted the sense of personal security of citizens in Western countries and changed the threat perspective of Western states" (Dauvergne 2007: 533). For the U.S. – Mexico border, the attacks meant that it had now become an important element of the U.S. led "War on Terrorism". It was widely believed that, unless action was taken quickly, another catastrophe on the order of September 11 was immanent (see Hayworth 2006). The majority of American citizens were, therefore, calling for enhanced homeland security measures, including heightened border protection (see Andreas 2003; Glon 2004; Tirman 2004).

Moreover, terrorism as a transnational security threat is, by its nature, "dependent on migration of people, weapons, information, and money" (Tirman 2004: 2). In this post-September 11 climate, (legal and illegal) immigrants soon came to be viewed with suspicion by both the government and many local communities. According to Walker, this climate was exacerbated by the fact that "citizens witness[ed] the effects of a porous border virtually every day and in practically every city – with the undocumented migrant population now above 11 million and spread across the continental United States" (2007: 137; see also Tirman 2004). The idea of "millions of illegal immigrants" flowing relatively uncontrolled into the United States from Mexico became an even more powerful theme than it had been before in American immigration policy (see Chavez 2008). Immigration control was now a critical national security priority (Andreas 2003; Walker 2007; Walters 2008; Romero 2008).

Once this link between immigration and national security was established, it was almost immediately followed by "a crackdown on movement across American borders" (Dauvergne 2007: 533). The undocumented immigrant in particular was no longer "just" seen as a "criminal alien," he was demonized as a "potential terrorist" (see Faist 2002). With an estimated 4 to 6 million immigrants clandestinely entering the United States each year, this was perceived as a problem (see Gilchrist & Corsi 2006). Soon after the attacks, terrorism policy, therefore, began to radically reshape immigration law and policy.

Just a little over one month after the attacks, President Bush signed into law the first of a series of Acts, which would ultimately inextricably link immigration with national security, i.e. terrorism. The *USA Patriot Act of 2001* significantly expanded the authority of the law enforcement agencies for the stated purpose of fighting terrorism (see Tirman 2004). It also enhanced surveillance and detention powers of the government with respect to non-citizens (see Tirman 2004). Over the next two years, the *Enhanced Border Security and Visa Entry Reform Act* (2002), the *Homeland Security Act* (2002), the *Aviation Transportation and Security Act* (2002), and the *Intelligence Reform and Terrorism Prevention Act* (2004) followed. All of these acts more or less expanded the authority of the law enforcement agencies and enhanced the agencies' surveillance and detention powers. The most prominent and controversial post-9/11 legislation, however, was probably the *Border Protection, Antiterrorism, and Illegal Immigration Control Act of 2005* (or so-called *Sensenbrenner Bill*). This bill is considered by immigrant rights groups to be "one of the most draconian in recent memory" (Doty 2007: 128). Although the bill was passed by the U.S. House of Representatives, it did not pass in the Senate. If it had, the bill would have made it a felony rather than a civil offense to be in the United States without authorization, required all employers to use an electronic database to verify employee's eligibility to be in the United States, authorized local law enforcement to enforce federal immigration laws, authorized a high-tech fence along sections of the southern border, and made it a criminal offense to come to the aid of migrants in distress. Albeit the bill being struck down, two of its provisions were realized otherwise. On September 14, 2006, the U.S. House of Representatives passed the *Secure Fence Act*, voting to build 700 miles of double-layered fencing which would cover over one-third of the almost 2,000-mile border. In addition to building the fence, the Act also requires the Department of Homeland Security (DHS) to install an intricate system of surveillance cameras along the Arizona-Mexico border. The second provision which was realized was the requirement that all employers use an electronic database to verify their potential employee's eligibility to be in the United States. In 2007, the federal government implemented the E-Verify system, which renders it possible for all employers to verify the legal status of every new employee hired. The program was set to expire in 2008 and many states have tried to pass their own legislation, making E-Verify background checks mandatory and imposing fines for employers who "knowingly" or "intentionally" hire workers without proper authorization (see e.g. Legal Arizona Workers Act 2007).[36]

Even though immigration and terrorism policy had to some extent overlapped even prior to 9/11, following the attacks this small overlap became near complete (see Tumlin 2004). "The new terrorism policy sends the message that immigrants of certain nationalities should be viewed as potential terror suspects first and as welcome newcomers second, if at all," says Karen C. Tumlin (2004: 1175). But that is not all. Since 9/11, federal antiterrorism efforts have increasingly used immigration laws as tools of investigation, prosecution, and prevention (see Tumlin 2004; Tirman 2004; Sheridan 2005; Meeropol 2006). For example, whereas terrorism charges can be difficult to prosecute, immigration laws have come to be seen as providing a quick and easy way to detain people who could be planning attacks (Sheridan 2005).

Furthermore, the events of September 11, 2001, not only prompted the allocation of more resources for border control, but also led to some major internal re-structuring of governmental institutions. For one, the DHS was created, resulting in the "largest government reorganization in contemporary history" (Romero 2008: 73; see also Tumlin 2004; Doty 2007). It replaced the INS, whose immigration-related responsibilities were transferred to the United States Customs and Immigration Service (U.S. CIS), a bureau of the DHS. The Immigration and Customs Enforcement (ICE) agency now oversees the enforcement of immigration law. Although the DHS's core mission was to fight terrorism, today it is very much involved in the prosecution of traditional immigration cases – even cases that appear to have relatively little to do with terrorism (see Doty 2007). For Tumlin, the abolition of the INS and the establishment of the DHS is "the clearest example of the way immigration and immigrant policy has been conflated with and subordinated to

---

[36] Several other bills had been proposed with the intent to reform immigration, such as the *Save America Comprehensive Immigration Reform Act of 2005*, the *Secure America and Orderly Immigration Act of 2005* or the *Comprehensive Immigration Reform Act of 2006*; though neither of these bills was passed in Congress.

terrorism policy goals" (2004: 1178). Secondly, the U.S. Customs and Border Protection agency was also restructured and became an agency within the DHS. Accordingly, its mission changed from formerly the interdiction of illegal drugs and regulation of trade, to a national security mission. Its primary mission is now to prevent terrorism and terrorist weapons from getting into the United States (see U.S. CBP-Strat. 2008; see also Andreas 2003). In addition to the link between immigration and terrorism, the extent of this re-structuring highlights the "unprecedented prominence" (Andreas 2003: 92) of law enforcement, including border control, on the post-September 11 security agenda. It also had profound symbolic impact, as it communicated the view that immigrants are potential terrorists.

Finally, the re-emergence of racial profiling in federal law enforcement since September 11 further consolidated this view. Racial profiling is "the most obvious way in which terrorism policy is driving immigration and immigrant policy," says Tumlin (2004: 1184). The new form of post-9/11 profiling, called "immigration-plus" profiling, is based on immigration status, national origin, and often presumed Muslim religion. "[I]mmigration status combined with a presumed Muslim identity serves as a proxy for terrorism danger; immigration status alone, without these nationality or religion plus factors, does not trigger heightened scrutiny," explains Tumlin (2004: 1184).[37] Although the United States had moved away from racial profiling or selectivity based on nationality since

---

[37] In practice, however, the profiling is not only used to identify immigrants from "al-Qaeda-designated nations". For example, the stated priority and purpose of the *Absconder Apprehension Initiative* is to locate and apprehend absconders from Muslim nations because, according to the Department of Justice (DOJ), they hail from countries where there has been an al-Qaeda presence. However, at the same time the DOJ admits that the overwhelming majority of the estimated 314,000 immigrants in the United States with final orders of deportation are Latin American, while less than 2% are actually from Muslim nations (see Tumlin 2004). These numbers, argues Tumlin, "contradict the DOJ's stated motive of addressing the problem of immigrants remaining in the country after receiving final orders of deportation" (2004: 1191). Such a policy, neutrally applied, she says, "would lead to mass deportations of a distinctly different set of immigrants" (2004: 1191). According to Tumlin (2004), this indicates that immigration status alone does not trigger government attention. Rather, the government is selectively enforcing immigration law based on national origin and presumed religion.

the 1960s, this changed again after the attacks. Ignoring both the over-inclusiveness (not all immigrants from al-Qaeda nations are terrorists) and under-inclusiveness (some terrorists are not immigrants and others are not from al-Qaeda nations) of this approach, the federal government quickly came to regard the use of immigration-plus profiling as essential in the fight against terrorism (see Tumlin 2004). This was widely supported by the American public. In fact, after 9/11, 70% of the population believed some type of profiling was essential to public security, whereas prior to 9/11, 80% had been opposed to it (Davis 2001).

Underpinning all of the decisions discussed above is the notion of the "illegal immigrant" as the "enemy," the "alien other," the potential terrorist. There is no doubt that the measures taken in response to the events of September 11, which were intended to "handle the threatening migrant" (Faist 2002: 12), have also made him or her more visible and exposed as an "alien". Tumlin sees a great danger in these developments because "allowing terrorism policy to become inextricably intertwined with immigration and immigrant policy threatens to undermine the ideas of equal justice and equal opportunity that represent the best of America" (2004: 1238). In a post-9/11 world, where "you are either with us or against us,"[38] this relationship "has all too easily been presumed" (Tumlin 2004: 1184).

It is precisely this presumption that the MCDC draws on. While the Minutemen regard "illegal immigration" as an enormous burden on America's health care, education, and welfare system, or voice concern about the effect that immigration has on American culture, it is the migrant as "potential terrorist" who expressly motivates their activities. "But [.] our biggest focus, of course, is ehm getting that border secured for national security and public safety," says the MCDC's Vice-President when asked about the organization's mission (Author Interview #1: 314-15). There are three ways in which the ("illegal") immigrant is perceived as a national security threat by the Minutemen.

First, the ("illegal") immigrant might come from a terror-friendly or terror-supporting country and try to clandestinely enter the United States by crossing the porous U.S. – Mexican border. Securing the border, the Vice-President says in her interview,

---

[38] Statement made by President Bush at a joint press conference with French President Jacques Chirac in November 2001 (see CNN 2001).

[is] an international problem. It's a *national* security problem...we have illegal aliens out of a hundred and forty-five [*] countries [trying to cross the border into the United States]. *Many* of them are coming from countries that are terrorist supporting (Author Interview #1: 680-83).

Every day, over one thousand "illegal" immigrants cross the 2,000-mile border between the United States and Mexico estimates the MCDC's Vice-President (see Author Interview #1). The first three years that the Minutemen were running shifts, Border Patrol was able to apprehend "over 4,000 illegal aliens" (Author Interview #1: 895) in one night, although they were only patrolling a stretch of maybe a half a mile. "So a loose stretch of a half a mile and *that* many people came across. And of course they didn't apprehend *all of them*," she adds (Author Interview #1: 890-95). Overall, the Vice-President believes that there are between thirty to forty million "illegal" immigrants living in the United States. Included in this estimate are many "illegal" immigrants from terror-supporting or terror-friendly countries (see Author Interviews #1, #2 and #3).

These circumstances lead the Minutemen to raise alarm that "America remains highly susceptible to another terrorist attack" (Glon 2004: 361). In their eyes, the border needs to be secured, because after 9/11 it was apparent that smugglers' methods, routes, and modes of transportation were potential vulnerabilities that could be exploited by terrorists and could result in terrorist weapons illegally entering the United States (see Minuteman website; see also Boudreaux & Schmitt 2004). Despite the fact that security analysts, academic scholars and news media alike presently agree that the picture of a U.S. – Mexican border primed for terrorism is "greatly exaggerated" (Walker 2007: 137; see also Ackleson 2005), the Minutemen are not deterred. Instead, the Minutemen have begun to build their own fence "to TRULY secure the border against events such as Pearl Harbor and 9/11" (MCDC 2008).

Simply building a better fence along the border, however, is not enough to keep potential terrorists from entering the United States. Terrorists are not limited to entering the United States by clandestinely crossing the southern border; they can, like most of the September 11 hijackers, enter on visas (see Author Interview #1 and #2). The fact that most of the 9/11 highjackers entered into the country legally is for the MCDC's

Vice-President only one more indication of "how broken our immigration system was" (Author Interview #1: 806).

Finally, potential terrorists not only illegally cross the border or legally enter on visa into the United States; some of them are, of course, already within the United States:

> And of course, we have plenty of terro- eh eh plenty of terrorist cells *within* the United States already. Many of them have already come through here. I don't think - you know the President always says, "It's been six years and we've not had another incident. The country has been protected." They're just waiting for the right time. I think they're here. And and they're - the next attack is being planned. They're just waiting for the right time. It's not because our President has protected us. No. Because if you think about it - I mean *now* - if you think about it it's six years after 9/11 and our borders are still wide open. You know (Author Interview #1: 817-31).

However, the Minutemen do not suggest what should happen with regard to this situation.

While the link between migration and security is not a new one, the attacks certainly added a new dimension to the debate about "illegal" immigration. They also heightened the public's awareness of and further inflated domestic anxieties about border security (Andreas 2003). As a consequence, the notion of "homeland security" quickly became part of everyday security discourse, and "illegal" immigration became inextricably linked to the debate about national security and terrorism prevention. In this post-9/11 climate, the MCDC was successfully able to link its own agenda with national security by drawing on the fears and the uncertainty that resulted from the attack (see also Doty 2007). In doing so, the events of September 11, 2001, in a way, functioned to energize and legitimize their activities.

11. Exceptionality and the Border

According to Giorgio Agamben (1998), at the heart of every democratic state operating under a declared rule of law, there exists the "state of exception," an emergency provision that empowers the state to act outside the constraints of law, permitting it to adopt extreme measures in its defense, including violence against its own citizens (see also Rosas 2006). It is the sovereign who has the ability to decide on this state of exception and to act exceptionally, which makes him a somewhat paradoxical figure because he is at the same time outside and inside the juridical order (see Agamben 1998).

Although Agamben himself does not situate his explanation for how and why there can be places of exception in a geographical context, Matthew Hannah (2008) tries to do so by linking sovereignty more explicitly with the problematic of territorial control. For Hannah, the sovereign's ability to decide on the state of exception presupposes the existence of a "person subject to and vulnerable to the sovereign's extralegal exception action" (2008: 60). If the sovereign's actions are to be effective in creating or restoring the social order, he argues, there must be embodied people vulnerable to becoming objects of these actions (Hannah 2008). But before these people can be stripped to what Agamben refers to as "bare life" or "sacred life" and can be placed into a space of exception, they must first be captured. Therefore, the main obstacle facing the organs of the state, and hence the main qualification to the assumption of sovereignty, is the lack of knowledge about the people who threaten the social order and where they are to be found (Hannah 2008). In this sense, undocumented immigration can be seen as an obstacle or even a threat to sovereignty (see also Beare 1999; Doty 1998; Doty 2007).

Indeed, once the clandestine movement of people becomes an issue, it quickly becomes a sovereignty issue because states generally claim the exclusive authority to decide who may enter and who may become a citizen (Weiner 1995; see also Beare 1999; Sassen 2000). In fact, the traditional sovereign state is considered the ultimate authority that can both impose and enforce order within a clearly demarcated territory, and defend its territory and its people against external threats (Axtmann 2004). For that reason, it seems natural that the state should feel particularly threatened when people are moving uncontrolled or even undetected "beyond the limits of the registered world" across borders (Hannah 2008:

71; see also Beare 1999). This was exemplified, when Ronald Reagan said in 1984 that no nation could lose control of its borders and still survive. In doing so, he transformed undocumented immigration "from a useful political issue into a more fundamental question of national security" (Durand et al. 1999: 521). By undermining the sovereignty of the state, undocumented immigration had now become a threat to the existence of the entire nation itself. As was shown, this shift was quickly responded to by increasingly militarized border law enforcement practices, exemplified through policing operations such as *Operations Hold the Line* and *Gatekeeper*. These operations positioned large numbers of Border Patrol agents along historically used migrant corridors in the hopes of preventing undocumented immigration through deterrence. Notably, similar tactics had been tried before, but they failed to capture policy makers' imaginations or garner public support until the eve of NAFTA (see Rosas 2006). At the same time that these enforcement efforts forced more and more migrants into dangerous forms of border crossing, charges of violence and harassment against immigration authorities also abounded. Soon, the decades-long construction of the "illegal immigrant" as a threat to American society together with its corresponding militarized law enforcement practices, created a situation in which the borderlands came to exemplify a "permanent state of racial emergency, or the permanent legal racial exception" (Rosas 2006: 337).

This situation was only exacerbated by the events of September 11, 2001, because almost over night they made the "enemy" very visible and easy to identify. Undocumented immigrants finally came to be seen as being "alien" in the sense of being different from the "legitimate" public (Beare 1999). In a way, they had been captured and now became those persons "subject to and vulnerable to the sovereign's extralegal exception action" (Hannah 2008: 60) whose existence the sovereign's ability to decide presupposes. From this perspective then, any exceptional legislation or police powers adopted to counter the immigrants' activities could now be decided on and argued to be justified due to the uniqueness of their threat and the imminent and existential danger it gave rise to (see Beare 1999; Doty 2007; Hannah 2008).

How does this relate to the emergence and legitimization of the MCDC? From the point of view of the Minutemen, the state failed to take these exceptional measures necessary in the aftermath of the September 11th, 2001, attacks. Despite the existence of an existential threat to the security of the American people, the government was "more concerned with securing the borders of foreign lands than securing the borders of the United States" (MCDC 2008). That the Minutemen arguably do perceive themselves as involved in a life and death struggle is evidenced by the rhetoric and imagery of war, which are ever-present. "[T]hese things do not constitute 'mere' metaphor and symbolism," says Doty; rather, they are "indications that the situation is perceived as one of threat with a very real element of risk" (2007: 125). But, as Doty (2007) correctly asks, what happens when it is perceived by a significant portion of the population that the sovereign does not in fact recognize the enemy, thus failing to distinguish friend from enemy and refusing to make the necessary decision?

Here, the doctrine of popular sovereignty comes into play. In the theoretical chapter of this book, popular sovereignty was introduced as the notion that no law or rule is legitimate unless it directly or indirectly rests on the consent of the people concerned. Although "the people" have placed their sovereign power in the hands of the state, they remain the ultimate and only legitimate basis for government (see Culberson 1990; Fritz 1994; Yack 2001; Axtmann 2004). Now the Minutemen, representing "the people," are demanding that the federal government "fulfil [its] constitutionally mandated responsibility" (MCDC 2008). This responsibility, as the (surrogate-) sovereign, is to protect its people from imminent, existential danger to the social order. However, the government seems unwilling or unable to do so. Thus, based on the notion that the law is made "by the people for the people," the Minutemen not only believe that it is their right but also their duty to fend for themselves. Ultimately, who makes the decision on the existence of the enemy and about the situation of imminent, existential danger to which this figure gives rise, is therefore a question of where sovereignty is located; and under the doctrine of popular sovereignty, it is located with the people.

Lastly, this supports the argument that the emergence of the MCDC cannot be explained simply in terms of the "War on Terror" and its legitimization of the policing of identities and nationalities. It must also be seen within the context of the decades-long construction of the U.S. – Mexican border as a place of danger and threat and of the Mexican immigrant as the poster child for "illegal immigration," the "illegal alien".

12. Globalization, Private Security and the Role of the State

Finally, this last chapter returns to Johnston's criminological definition of vigilantism. According to Johnston (1996), vigilantism is not merely a synonym for social control. Rather, it is a popularly initiated strategy, arising as a reaction to social deviance (real, threatened or imputed), whose aim is to offer people the assurance that an established system of order will prevail. The existence of a real or perceived threat alone, however, is not sufficient to trigger the emergence of vigilantism. If, in addition to the threat, the government fails to satisfactorily control those who pose the threat, then vigilantism is said to emerge.

Previously, it was shown how the MCDC has constructed the ("illegal") immigrant as a threat to America's national security. In the following, a brief and rather explorative look will be taken at two interconnected societal transformations which, it is argued, provide a useful insight as to why the Minutemen perceive the government as inefficient: first, globalization with its associated forces of political and economic liberalization; and second, the privatization of security and the rise of responsible citizenship. Due to the spatial and temporal constraints of this project, this topic is only explored with tentative brevity.

12.1 Globalization and Border Control

Importantly, we are living in an era of globalization and regional economic integration "defined by a loosening of controls over legitimate cross-border exchange" (Andreas 1999: 592). But although free trade and the free flow of capital are advocated as a means of providing for efficient resource allocation to the benefit of all, the same does not apply to the free movement of people (Weiner 1995; Revelli 2008). At the same time that borders are being effaced in order to facilitate greater economic mobility, security concerns about "porous borders" are leading to what Rumford calls a "securitized re-bordering" (2006: 157) of states who wish to better control flows of migrant workers, refugees and terrorists (see also Beare 1999; Andreas 2003). Especially in a post-9/11 environment, finding a balance between these two interests is an ever-growing challenge because there are limits to how much states can seal their borders if they wish to maintain a legitimate cross-border exchange (Andreas 2003). If all three NAFTA partners want to continue to benefit from an interdependent regional economy, the border must remain economically open, although Mexico and Canada are arguably much more dependent on trade with the United States than the other way around.

Regardless of the degree of this interdependency though, as a result of it, and this was shown in more detail earlier in this thesis, the United States' stance toward immigration and border control almost always has shifted in accordance with the country's economic interests and needs. This indicates that the federal government ambitiously has tried and continues to try to have it both ways; the latest indication of this being the *Smart Border Agreement* passed in 2002. Rather than giving up any pretence of controlling borders, or simply shutting down borders in the name of security and "accepting the astronomical costs," the government seeks to create "borders that perform as better security barriers and as efficient economic bridges at the same time" (Andreas 2003: 96). This, however, can easily lead to seemingly volatile and ineffective policymaking.

12.2 Globalization and Security

What is more, for almost two centuries, the territorially consolidated, centralized sovereign state was regarded as the ultimate power that could impose, and enforce, order (see Garland 2001; Krahmann 2003; Axtmann 2004; Stenson & Lea 2007). According to Axtmann (2004), the success of this sovereign state rested on the acceptance of its claim to be able to guarantee the physical security, the economic well-being, and the cultural identity of its citizens (see also Stenson & Lea 2007). Today, state authorities are progressively turning to the resources and expertise of non-state organizations and actors when it comes to the provision of security. "Instead of imagining they can monopolize crime control, or exercising their sovereign powers in complete disregard of the powers of other actors, state agencies now adopt a strategic relation to other forces of social control," writes David Garland, "They seek to build broader alliances, enlisting the 'governmental' powers of private actors, and shaping them to the ends of crime control" (2001: 124; see also O'Connor et al. 2008). Ultimately, it is hoped that this will create an "enhanced network of more or less directed, more or less informal crime control, complementing and extending the formal controls of the criminal justice state"

(Garland 2001: 124). This form of governing-at-a-distance, however, not only spreads responsibility for crime control onto agencies, organizations and individuals that operate outside the criminal justice state, it encourages these non-governmental actors to actively engage with this greater responsibility (see Johnston 2001; Garland 2001; Stenson & Lea 2007). In part, this transformation in the governance and provision of security is attributable to globalization with its associated forces of political and economic liberalization.

12.2.1 Risk Society

Globalization can and does create risks. It can shake the foundations of established institutions and undermine the existence of traditional economies (Bislev 2004). The security implications of this so-called postmodern shift are for Sven Bislev (2004) exemplified in Ulrich Beck's formulation of the idea of a "risk society". Beck (1992) argues that postmodern society is a society organized in response to risk. The type of risk that this society is exposed to, Beck says, emerges as the result of the modernization process itself as technological innovation proceeds. At the same time that technological innovation proceeds, it not only makes unskilled and uneducated labor increasingly superfluous, but gives rise to newly manufactured risks that were unknown before. Since these risks are the product of human activity, however, they can be monitored, assessed, predicted and possibly prevented. These risks (or insecurities) and their associated security technologies, he argues, constitute a new structuring principle in western society (Beck 1992).

In addition to the structures and institutions of society, processes, i.e. practices and discourses, also change in response to these manufactured risks (Bislev 2004; see also Amoore & de Goede 2008; Zedner 2009). In numerous areas of social life, risk and security discourses come to dominate the public space. The new "governmentality" expressed in these discourses represents a shift from welfare-state to risk-society governance (see Bislev 2004; Garland 2001; Inda 2006; Amoore & de Goede 2008). The resulting social fragmentation (risk, like wealth, is distributed unevenly in society), Pratten and Sen argue, "creates uncertainty and rootlessness and alienates categories of the vulnerable – the deskilled, the part-time, immigrants and unemployed" (2008: 3). As was shown previously, the security discourse particularly has specific political effects:

securitization leads to the legitimization of measures that would not have been possible had the discourse not taken the form of existential threats and made a claim to be about security.

When it comes to crime control, the risk perspective changes the way offenders are perceived. As Garland puts it, offenders "rather than as clients in need of support are seen as risks that must be managed" (2001: 175). In order to manage the risk posed by the offender, he is now broken up into a set of measurable risk factors (see Valverde & Mopas 2004; Zedner 2009). This drive towards managerial accountability ultimately leads toward an understanding of justice and security, which emphasizes economy, efficiency, and effectiveness in the use of resources (see Garland 2001; Zedner 2009). Almost naturally, then, this understanding promotes the collaboration among a growing range of public and private security actors for the management of risk and the provision of security. While the sovereign state was traditionally seen as the entity that guaranteed the security of its citizens, security has now become a commodity that can be purchased from a range of alternative options, the state being just one of those options (see Johnston 1996; Johnston & Shearing 2003; Zedner 2009). Once security becomes a commodity, however, it also becomes liable to give rise to "huge disparities in the social provision and distribution of security" (Garland 1996: 463) because it is distributed by market forces rather than according to need. Garland (1996) concludes that this kind of risk-based management and policing of crime ultimately shifts the burden of social control on to individuals and organizations. Communities are now urged to take any kind of risk information provided to them by the government and take their own precautions for their safety and the safety of their neighborhoods (see also Valverde & Mopas 2004). It seems not too far-fetched to conclude that this form of "responsibilization" and active engagement of private actors in the provision of security can create the impression that the state alone is incapable of effectively providing security, law and order, and crime control within its territorial boundaries. Indeed, scholarly discussions whether we are witnessing a weakening of the state or merely a re-articulation of relations between state and non-state actors abound (see Crawford 1997; Abrahams 1998; Bayley & Shearing 2001; Stenson & Lea 2007).

12.2.2 The MCDC and Responsibilization

Reflecting the aforementioned line of argument, Walker (2007) *inter alia* attributes the emergence of border vigilantism to the publication of the 9/11 Commission Report. He argues that the 9/11 Commission Report engaged the public, and arguably the vigilantes, in the problems at America's borders in such a way that it made American citizens feel responsible for enforcing the borders themselves in the absence of the government's willingness to do so. The Commission had been appointed by President Bush in the aftermath of the events of September 11th, 2001, to investigate the attacks. When the Commission released its findings in July 2004, it found that:

> More than 500 million people annually cross U.S. borders at legal entry points, about 330 million of them noncitizens. Another 500,000 or more enter illegally without inspection across America's thousands of miles of land borders or remain in the country past the expiration of their permitted stay. The challenge for national security in an age of terrorism is to prevent the very few people who may pose overwhelming risks from entering or remaining in the United States undetected (The 9/11 Commission Report 2004).

From this followed three recommendations (see Walker 2007). First, the Commission stressed the importance of travelling across American borders. It suggested that the United States combine intelligence, operations, and law enforcement in a strategy to intercept and constrain terrorist mobility. Second, the Commission underscored the need to integrate border control with infrastructure (so-called integrated border management).[39] "The U.S. border security system should be integrated into a larger network of screening points that includes the nation's transportation system and access to vital facilities, such as nuclear reactors," read the Report. Third, it recommended that the DHS, properly supported by the Con-

---

[39] For more information on this new form of border management, see e.g. Koslowski (2006).

gress, should complete, as quickly as possible, a biometric entry-exit screening system.[40]

Each of these recommendations called on Congress to increase border security. Then, when it appeared that Congress did not adequately respond to these public calls for reform, border vigilantism emerged as "the self-appointed private alternative for border enforcement" (Walker 2007: 146). Indeed, this argument seems to find some support, when the MCDC's Vice-President explains:

> [I]f you leave the –e from the word "vigilante," vigilant that's what the President asked us to do: to be vigilant and to report any suspicious activity after 9/11. And that's exactly what we do. We just answered the call that he *put out*, you know. *He* put out a call to the American public. And so that's what we did (Author Interview #1: 1060-66).

By engaging the public as a whole in the "War on Terror," every citizen was suddenly responsible for the security of the nation. The federal government clearly had sent a message that in this war it alone was not, and could not, effectively be responsible for preventing terrorists from entering the United States and carrying out future attacks.

---

[40] The first step toward the implementation of such a system was taken on the day of the attacks with the *National Security Entry-Exit Registration program* (NSEER). NSEER developed the first biometric database of "risky aliens" (Epstein 2008: 181), by combining a new, biometrics-based registration process for travellers to the US who are deemed potentially risky, with pre-existing databases that already used biometrics (see Epstein 2008). NSEER was terminated in December, 2003, and then progressively replaced by the *United States Visitor and Immigration Status Indicator Technology* (US VISIT). US VISIT is the most extensive application of the new biometric technologies to date. For a very insightful analysis of this particular convergence of state and new technology and the way it has impacted on contemporary border protection practices, as well as an analysis of the way the use of these new biometric technologies can be read from the logic of the contemporary state, see Epstein (2008).

PART III: SUMMARY AND CONCLUSION

> On the one hand, states are saturated in self-imaginings grounded in the law…On the other hand, we witness the deregulation and decentralization of the law predicated on the ideology and practice of "outsourcing" life services to the market….This twilight space accommodates a "culture of productive deception" and an elision of the law and lawlessness. Betwixt and between an alternative citizenry "stand in" for the state, conversant in "languages of stateness," and able to represent the state precisely because it moves with impunity between appeals to the form of law and forms of extra-judicial practice that are clearly construed as lying, outside or prior to the state.
>
> ~ Pratten & Sen 2008:4

13. Summary

In the United States, vigilantism is not a new phenomenon. To the contrary, America has a long-standing vigilante tradition. The second part of this research showed that time and again vigilante movements have emerged and have played an integral part in American history and culture (see Brown 1976; Abrahams 1998; Chacón & Davis 2007).

Since September 11, 2001, the United States has witnessed the (re-) emergence of civilian groups "taking the law into their own hands" in order to secure America's borders against "illegal immigrants" and potential terrorists. Initially brushed aside by politicians as little more than vigilantes "far outside the mainstream of public opinion," they have managed to generate incredible media coverage and their persistence on this issue has more than ever turned public attention to America's permeable borders and to the "failure" of the federal government in protecting its own country against terrorist threats. The Minuteman Civil Defense Corps is by far the largest, most active, and arguably most influential of these civilian border patrols.

Despite the MCDC's apparent influence and the tremendous amount of media coverage it receives, it was shown that only very few academic researchers have approached the Minuteman phenomenon thus far (Walker 2007; Doty 2007; Chavez 2007; Chacón & Davis 2007). As was stated in the introduction, Doty (2007) and Chavez (2007) have suggested that the emergence of the MCDC can be attributed to the decades-long public discourse in the United States that has constructed and represented the U.S. – Mexican border as a place of danger and a threat to American society and culture. Chavez even sees the Minutemen's enlistment of citizens to patrol the border as a "logical consequence" (2008: 34) of these discourses. On the other hand, the global (re-) emergence of vigilantism generally, has been linked by Pratten and Sen (2008) to globalization and its associated forces of political and economic liberalization.

What had not been done so far was to analyze the emergence of the MCDC more thoroughly by taking a broader and comprehensive look at the societal transformations which accompanied its emergence. This research explored why the MCDC emerged and why it emerged at this particular moment in time. It did so, firstly, by exploring how the gradual securitization of immigration (which received additional impetus through the events of September 11th, 2001) established the "illegal immigrant" as a threat to America's national security; and secondly, by showing how globalization has transformed the traditional security landscape in such a manner that it tolerates and, arguably, even encourages citizens to take the law into their own hands.

In the third part of this work, a closer look was taken at the history of immigration control in the United States. It was argued that U.S. immigration policies and prevention techniques not only failed to prevent undocumented immigration across the border, but also succeeded in establishing the border as a place of danger and threat. The history of the border and of Mexican immigration to the United States has been mostly cyclical in nature. Over the years, phases of inclusion alternated with phases of exclusion, deportation, and often violence (see Tichenor 1994; Tichenor 2002; Rodriguez 2006; Ruiz 2006; Walker 2007). To a large extent, this fluctuation was due to the economics of migration. Whenever migration was regarded as "good for the country," that is, when the undocumented immigrant was seen to be necessary or beneficial, for example during labor shortages, it was tolerated and not much of a public "issue". Once conditions changed, however, this tolerance was quickly replaced with targeted enforcement practices (see Beare 1999; Tichenor 2002). Frequently, these enforcement practices not only channeled the clandestine border crossers to the most dangerous and remote regions of the border; but it also led to many small towns along the border feeling overrun by immigrants almost over night (see Ellingwood 2004). Especially the later exclusionary phases were, therefore, often accompanied by calls for a strong rule of law, heightened national security, and perhaps anti-immigrant sentiments, such as xenophobia or nativism - three themes which Walker (2007) has also identified as motivating contemporary border vigilante movements (see also Tichenor 2002).

Moreover, it was shown that while the early Mexican worker was described as "docile, patient, usually orderly in camp, fairly intelligent under competent supervision, obedient, and cheap" (Reisler 1976: 232) and was regarded as a great source of cheap labor, this changed as Mexican immigrants became increasingly urbanized and dispersed geographically. At that point, Americans gradually began to grow conscious of the "alien tide" from below the border, and the "illegal immigrant" soon became the "invisible enemy in their midst". This perception was exacerbated further not only by the "War on Drugs" and its attendant militarization of the border, but also through official discourses lamenting that control over the border was lost. Ever since, the "illegal immigrant" has been connected symbolically with invaders, criminals, and drug smugglers, "pictured as poised menacingly along a lightly defended two-thousand-mile frontier dividing the United States from Mexico and the poor masses of the Third World" (Durand et al. 1999: 521).

Based on the interview data, this research then illustrated how these images of the "illegal immigrant" as a threat to national security are reflected in the discursive practices of the Minutemen today and are regarded as motivating their activities. In particular with regard to the events of September 11th, 2001, it was discussed how official responses to the attacks served to reinforce the migration-security nexus, and how the Minutemen were successfully able to link their anti-immigrant agenda to the ensuing debate about national security. This, it is argued, gave the MCDC the energy and legitimization to become as large and as influential as it is today.

Secondly, a brief and explorative look was taken at recent changes in the way security is produced and "guaranteed" by the state. It was argued that whereas traditionally the sovereign state has been seen as the sole provider of law and order for its citizens, increasing privatization in the security sector has given rise to a feeling of government unwillingness or inability to effectively deal with perceived threats. It was discussed how, as a result of this transformation in the security sector, traditional distinctions between private and public, centralized and decentralized increasingly become blurred and private citizens are even encouraged to engage in a variety of productive security activities themselves. For the vigilantes this means the government is perceived as no longer being able to give its citizens the security "guarantees" they need, and they have emerged to temporarily "stand in" for the state in its absence.

Coupling this with the decades-long discursive construction of security both in terms of migration and terrorism at the U.S. – Mexican border, which, at minimum has increased U.S. perceptions of risks, danger, and security, vigilantism almost appears as a "logical response" (Pratten & Sen 2008: 2).

14. Conclusion

Vigilantism is a fascinating and difficult subject to study. It is elusive, enigmatic, paradoxical and amorphous. At times, it is difficult to delineate from other movements of extra-legal violence. The lines of demarcation are not always clearly drawn. Vigilantism is not a geographically fixed, historically specific phenomenon; yet its emergence cannot be understood without taking into account its social, cultural, and historical context. In fact, it was shown that the pressing imperatives behind vigilante violence are often long historical trajectories and particular cultural repertoires, as Pratten and Sen (2008) suggest. Vigilantism is global. Vigilantes have arisen at many times in different regions of the world as "defenders, often by force, of their view of the good life against those they see to be its enemies" (Abrahams 1998: 1). Vigilantism also reveals some of the fundamental ambiguities in relations between people and the state (see Abrahams 1998). Lastly, vigilantism all too frequently carries the "added onus of nativism, class prejudice, political motivation or personal ambition" (Caughey 1960: 13).

Although, or because, this book has presented a first explorative and at times tentative look at the emergence of the MCDC, many important questions regarding these civilian groups remain which either deserve closer scrutiny or have not been touched upon at all in this work.

For one, the discussion presented in this thesis is based only on three interviews. For a more complete representation, further interviews could be conducted with higher ranking members of the MCDC in states other than Arizona, as well as with regular volunteers attending border shifts or MCDC events. On the one hand, this might prove insightful when trying to understand who the leaders and followers of such vigilante organizations are and what motivates them to start/run or participate in such an organization; on the other, it could also be learned more about the various roles or functions that volunteers in the organization perform or what qualities help an individual, for example, to be an effective vigilante leader.

Similarly, it would be interesting to examine more closely the actual impact the Minutemen have on immigration policy and on the lives of immigrants subjected to those policies. Further insight might be gained from studying the MCDC in relation to other anti-immigrant movements, such as hate or white supremacist groups. Still little is known about exactly how, when, and why anti-immigrant sentiments, which are almost always present, metamorphose into coherent and powerful movements that, at the very least, threaten the civil liberties, the personal safety, and sometimes even the right of the immigrants to live in the United States. Existing literature on vigilantism and militia movements, suggests that this is somehow related to real or perceived social and political crises and/or major structural change in society. The findings in this thesis seem to some degree to support this, though – at least for the case of vigilantism – explaining its uprising solely in terms of major social disruptions seems to oversimplify the phenomenon.

The emergence and existence of the MCDC also raises several theoretical and conceptual issues and questions. As was mentioned previously, in their recent book *Global Vigilantes* David Pratten and Atreyee Sen (2008) connect the global (re-) emergence of vigilantism to globalization and its associated forces of political and economic liberalization. The transformation in the governance of security based on economic principles, Pratten and Sen argue, creates unparalleled opportunities and motives for citizens to take the law into their own hands.

Just probing into this matter in the last chapter of this thesis, makes it sufficiently clear that Pratten and Sen make a very valid argument; and certainly one that deserves more careful analysis with regard to the MCDC. If the Minutemen are indeed as influential as they themselves suggest, the emergence and practice of their organization raises important questions with regard to the state and its role in the production of security. Have the Minutemen truly emerged as a result of this new paradigm shift towards privatization in the governance of security? If yes, then what are the implications for the traditional understanding of the state's provision of security, its monopoly of force, as the essential function of government? Is the legitimacy which the Minutemen have gained indicative of a weakening of the state or is it merely the result of a re-articulation of relations between state and non-state actors?

Moreover, Abrahams (1998) argues that vigilantes present themselves as a "stop-gap," temporarily standing in for the state, rather than as a permanent replacement for malfunctioning state institutions. In light of recent trends toward the gradual privatization and outsourcing of security, it begs the question whether this still holds true. Ultimately, however, it begs the question about the function of vigilantism. Does vigilantism fulfill a socially constructive or a socially destructive function? Addressing this question would require an assessment of the impact the MCDC has had not only on the lives of immigrants, but also on the lives of citizens of either nation living in the border region. If the Minutemen are indeed successful in providing security "guarantees" to citizens and participants alike, this would surely be indicative of a socially stabilizing and constructive rather than a destructive function and vice versa. Although this certainly also depends on who is asked.

Finally, if one were to allow citizens to patrol the U.S. – Mexican border, for example by deputizing them or allowing them to become a *posse*, under which circumstances and conditions could this or should this be done? Certainly, as Walker (2007) writes, in this case it would be imperative to define clearly the rights and responsibilities of such vigilante groups, and to balance their ability to freely associate and patrol the border with the individual rights to due process and the basic human rights, dignity, and safety of the migrants.

Whether the emergence of the MCDC can really be attributed to one decisive moment in time, such as to the events of September 11, 2001, is doubtful. If this thesis has shown one thing, then it is what kind of an elusive and complex phenomenon vigilantism really is, and how many different aspects must be considered when one truly wants to understand why it arises at a certain time and a certain place. Even then the phenomenon remains too closely tied to cultural, legal, political and historical specificities to make any findings generalizable. The fact that there have been no reported incidences of civilians patrolling the Canadian border in a similar fashion, and, as was shown, the historical and economic uniqueness of the U.S. – Mexican borderlands, suggest that a generalization possibly even across the United States cannot be made.

It does seem plausible to say that major transformations in society, resulting in social or political upheaval, can create an environment in which the potential for the emergence of vigilantism increases. Literature on social movements more generally certainly seems to indicate that this is so. A look at the history of vigilantism or at the rise and fall of anti-immigrant sentiment over time, for the United States at least, also offers some support for this theory. Nonetheless, it is impossible to establish a direct causal relationship between the two, which again supports the argument that there is more to vigilantism than meets the eye at first glance. Sometimes just one charismatic leader may be enough. At other times, the interplay of multiple factors is decisive.

For the case of the Minutemen, the events of September 11th, 2001, have certainly enabled them to link their agenda to national security discourses in the United States, which to some degree has functioned to energize and legitimize their activities. It has definitely, in the very least, made sure that they received the media attention they were seeking. Whether national security is truly the motivating factor behind their emergence, is uncertain. In the interviews, more concern was shown about the social and cultural changes that immigrants may bring to America than about immigrant terrorists. And while the MCDC's Vice-President calls herself "the chosen one" and believes herself to be on a divine mission, the other two interviewees appeared less ideologically but rather opportunistically motivated.

Bibliography

Abrahams, Ray (1998). *Vigilant Citizens and the State,* Cambridge: Polity Press.

Agamben, Giorgio (1998). *Homo Sacer: Sovereign Power and Bare Life*, Palo Alto: Stanford University Press.

Alvarez, Robert R. (1994). The Mexican-US Border: The Making of an Anthropology of Borderlands, *Annual Review of Anthropology,* 24: 447-470.

Andreas, Peter (2003). Redrawing the Line: Borders and Security in the Twenty-First Century, *International Security,* 28(2): 78-111.

Andreas, Peter and Richard Price (2001). From War Fighting to Crime Fighting: Transforming the American National Security State, *International Studies Review,* 3(3): 31-52.

Andreas, Peter (1996). U.S. - Mexico: Open Markets, Closed Border, *Foreign Policy,* 103: 51-69.

Anthony, Joe (2005). Vigilantes Patrol US Border: The Politics of the Minuteman Project. (http://www.wsws.org/articles/2005/may2005/minu-m20.shtml; last visited on 26 September 2008).

Archibold, Randal C. (2006). A Border Watcher Finds Himself Under Scrutiny, *The New York Times,* 24 November 2006. (http://www.nytimes.com/2006/11/24/us/24border.html; last visited on 26 September 2008).

Axtmann, Roland (2004). The State of the State: The Model of the Modern State and its Contemporary Transformation, *International Political Science Review,* 25(3): 259-279.

Bacon, David (2007). The Real Political Purpose of the ICE Raids, *Dollars & Sense.*

(http://www.dollarsandsense.org/archives/2007/0507bacon.html; last visited on 26 September 2008).

Baker, Susan G. (1997). The "Amnesty" Aftermath: Current Policy Issues Stemming from the Legalization Programs of the 1986 Immigration Reform and Control Act, *International Migration Review*, 31(1): 5-27.

Bayley, David and Clifford Shearing (2001). *The New Structure of Policing: Description, Conceptualization, and Research Agenda*, Washington, D.C.: National Institute of Justice.

Batalova, Jeanne (April 2008). Mexican Immigrants in the United States. (http://www.migrationinformation.org/USfocus/display.cfm?id=679; last visited 15 September 2008).

Baum, Dan (2006). Patriots on the Borderline, *Los Angeles Times Magazine*, 16 March 2006. (http://www.latinamericanstudies.org/immigration/borderline.htm ; last visited on 26 September 2008).

Beare, Margaret E. (1999). Illegal Migration: Personal Tragedies, Social Problems, or National Security Threats?" in: Phil Williams (ed.), *Illegal Immigration and Commercial Sex. The New Slave Trade*, London: Frank Cass.

Beck, Ulrich (1992). *Risk Society*, London: Sage Publications.

Bersin, Alan D. (1996). El Tercer País: Reinventing the U.S./Mexico Border, *Stanford Law Review*, 48(5): 1413-1420.

Bislev, Sven (2004). Globalization, State Transformation, and Public Security, *International Political Science Review*, 25: 281-296.

Boudreaux, Richard and Richard B. Schmitt (2004). U.S. Fears Terrorism Via Mexico's Time-Tested Smuggling Routes, *The Los Angeles Times*, 15 September 2004.

(http://articles.latimes.com/2004/sep/15/nation/na-mexterror15; last visited on 05 October 2008).

Brooks, Karen. (2005). Citizen Patrols Try to Shed Vigilante Image, *Dallas Morning News*, 8 November 2005.

Brown, Richard Maxwell. (1975). *Strain of Violence: Historical Studies of American Violence and Vigilantism*, New York: Oxford University Press.

Burrows, William. (1976). *Vigilante!* New York: Harcourt Brace Publishers.

Bustamante, Jorge A. (1992). Demystifying the United States-Mexico Border, *The Journal of American History*, 79(2): 485-490.

Buzan, Barry, Ole Waever and Jaap de Wilde (1998). Security. A New Framework for Analysis, Boulder: 1998.

Camarota, Steven A. (November 2007). Immigrants in the United States, 2007. A Profile of America's Foreign-Born Population. (http://www.cis.org/articles/2007/back1007.pdf; last visited on 18 August 2008).

Camarota, Steven A. (August 2007). 100 Million More. Projecting the Impact of Immigration on the U.S. Population, 2007 to 2060. (http://www.cis.org/articles/2007/back707.html; last visited on 18 August 2008).

Chacón, Justin Akers and Mike Davis (2007). *No One is Illegal: Fighting Racism and State Violence on the U.S.-Mexico Border*, Chicago: Haymarket Books.

Chavez, Leo (2008). Spectacle in the Desert: The Minuteman Project on the US-Mexico Border, in: David Pratten and Atreyee Sen (eds.) (2008). *Global Vigilantes*, New York: Columbia University Press: 25-46.

Chiswick, Barry R. (1988). Illegal Immigration and Immigration Control, *The Journal of Economic Perspectives,* 2(3): 101-115.

Church, George J. (1984). 'We are overwhelmed', *TIME,* 25 June 1984. (http://www.time.com/time/magazine/article/0,9171,926593,00.html; last visited on 26 September 2008).

Conover, Ted (1997). Border Vigilantes, *The New York Times,* 11 May 1997. (http://query.nytimes.com/gst/fullpage.html?res=9904E1D61F31F932A25756C0A961958260&scp=6&sq=immigration%20mexico%20vigilante&st=cse; last visited on 26 September 2008).

Cornelius, Wayne A. (2001). Death at the Border: Unintended Consequences of US Immigration Control Policy, *Population and Development Review,* 27(4): 661-685.

Crawford, Adam (1997). *The Local Governance of Crime: Appeals to Community and Partnerships,* Oxford: Clarendon Press.

Crawford, Adam, Stuart Lister, Sarah Blackburn and Jonathan Burnett (2005). *Plural Policing: The Mixed Economy of Visible Security Patrols,* Bristol: Policy Press.

Dauvergne, Catherine (2007). Security and Migration Law in the Less Brave New World, *Social & Legal Studies,* 16: 533-549.

Davis, Nicole (2001). The Slippery Slope of Racial Profiling, *ColorLines,* 05 December 2001. (http://www.arc.org/C_Lines/CLArchive/story2001_12_05.html; last visited on 25 September 2008).

DePalma, Anthony (1995). Mexico and U.S. to Patrol Border Trouble Spots, *The New York Times,* 27 October 1995. (http://query.nytimes.com/gst/fullpage.html?res=990CE7D71531F934A15753C1A963958260&scp=29&sq=immigration%20mexico%20vigilante&st=cse; last visited on 21 September 2008).

Doty, Roxanne Lynn (2007). States of Exception on the Mexico-U.S. Border: Security, 'Decisions,' and Civilian Border Patrols, *International Political Sociology*, 1: 113-37.

Doty, Roxanne Lynn (1998). Immigration and the Politics of Security, *Security Studies*, 8(2):71-93.

Dowd, Maureen (1983). Losing Control of the Borders, *TIME*, 13 June 1983. (http://www.time.com/time/magazine/article/0,9171,952001,00.html; last visited on 26 September 2008).

Durand, Jorge, Douglas Massey and Emilio Parrado (1999). The New Era of Mexican Migration to the United States, *The Journal of American History*, 86(2): 518-536, Special Issue: Rethinking History and the Nation-State: Mexico and the United States as a Case Study.

Eschbach, Karl, Jacqueline Hagan, Nestor Rodriguez, Ruben Hernandez-Leon and Stanley Bailey (1999). Death at the Border, *International Migration Review*, 33(2): 430-454.

Espenshade, Thomas J. (1995). Unauthorized Immigration to the United States, *Annual Review of Sociology*, 21: 195-216.

Espenshade, Thomas J. (1994). Does the Threat of Border Apprehension Deter Undocumented US Immigration? *Population and Development Review*, 20(4): 871-892.

Faist, Thomas (2002). 'Extension du domaine de la lutte': International Migration and Security before and after September 11, 2001, *International Migration Review*, 36(1): 7-14.

Freilich, Joshua, Jeremy Pienik and Gregory Howard (2001). Toward Comparative Studies of the U.S. Militia Movement, *International Journal of Comparative Sociology*, 42: 163-210.

Fritz, Christian G. (1994). Popular Sovereignty, Vigilantism, and the Constitutional Right of Revolution, *The Pacific Historical Review*, 63(1): 39-66.

Garland, David (2001). *The Culture of Control. Crime and Social Order in Contemporary Society*, Oxford: Oxford University Press.

Garland, David (1996). The Limits of the Sovereign State. Strategies of Crime Control in Contemporary Society, *The British Journal of Criminology*, 36(4): 445-471.

Gerstle, Gary (2004). The Immigrant as Threat to American Security: A Historical Perspective, in: John Tirman (ed). *The Maze of Fear: Security and Migration after 9/11*, New York: New Press: 87-108.

Gilchrist, Jim and Jerome Corsi (2006). *Minutemen: The Battle to Secure America's Borders*, Los Angeles: World Ahead Publishing.

Gwynne, S.C. (1994). The Unwelcome Mat, *TIME*, 28 November 1994. (http://www.time.com/time/magazine/article/0,9171,981902,00.html; last visited on 26 September 2008).

Hannah, Matthew G. (2008). Spaces of Exception and Unexceptionability, in: Deborah Cowen and Emily Gilbert (eds). *War, Citizenship, Territory*, New York: Routledge.

Hanson, Gordon and Antonio Spilimbergo (1999). Illegal Immigration, Border Enforcement, and Relative Wages: Evidence from Apprehensions at the U.S.-Mexico Border, *The American Economic Review*, 89(5):1337-1357.

Hayworth, John David and Joseph Eule (2006). *Whatever It Takes: Illegal Immigration, Border Security and the War on Terror*, Washington, D.C.: Regnery Publishing, Inc.

Hernández, Kelly Lytle (2006). The Crimes and Consequences of Illegal Immigration: A Cross-Border Examination of Operation Wetback, 1943-1954, *The Western Historical Quarterly*, 37(4): 421-444.

Hoefer, Michael, Nancy Rytina and Christopher Campbell (2007). Estimates of the Unauthorized Immigrant Population Residing in the United States: January 2006, Office of Immigration Statistics, Department of Homeland Security. (http://www.dhs.gov/xlibrary/assets/statistics/publications/ill_pe_2006.pdf; last visited on 18 August 2008).

Horwitz, Tony (2006). Immigration — and the Curse of the Black Legend, *The New York Times*, 9 July 2006. (http://www.nytimes.com/2006/07/09/opinion/09horwitz.html?scp=13&sq=immigration%20mexico%20vigilante&st=cse; last visited on 26 September 2008).

Huntington, Samuel (2004). *Who Are We? America's Great Debate*, London: Free Press.

Huntington, Samuel (2000). The Special Case of Mexican Immigration: Why Mexico is a Problem, *The American Enterprise*, 20-22.

Jamail, Milton H. (1981). Voluntary Organizations Along the Border, *Proceedings of the Academy of Political Science*, 34 (1):78-87, Special Issue: Mexico-United States Relations.

Johnson, David A. (1981). Vigilance and the Law: The Moral Authority of Popular Justice in the Far West, *American Quarterly*, 33(5): 558-586, Special Issue: American Culture and the American Frontier.

Johnston, Les (2001). Crime, Fear and Civil Policing, *Urban Studies*, 38(5-6): 959-976.

Johnston, Les (1996). What is Vigilantism? *British Journal of Criminology*, 36: 220-236.

Jordan, Lara Jakes (2005). 'Minutemen' to Patrol Arizona Border – Civilians plan to patrol a 40-mile stretch of the southeast Arizona, *The Sacramento Union*, 21 February 2005. (http://www.sacunion.com/pages/nation/articles/minutemen_to_patrol_arizona_border/ ; last visited on 19 August 2008).

Kirchner, Emil J. (2007). Regional and global security. Changing threats and institutional responses, in: Emil Kirchner and James Sperling (eds.). *Global Security Governance. Competing perceptions of security in the 21st century*, New York: Routledge: 3-22.

Kowalewski, David (1996). Countermovement Vigilantism and Human Rights: A Propositional Inventory, *Crime, Law and Social Change*, 25(1): 63-81.

Krahmann, Elke (2003). Conceptualizing Security Governance, *Cooperation and Conflict*, 38: 5-26.

Levinson, Sanford (2002). Arms, Right To Bear, in: Kermit L. Hall (ed). *The Oxford Guide to American Law*, New York: Oxford University Press: 35-36.

Mabee, Bryan (2003). Security Studies and the 'Security State': Security Provision in Historical Context, *International Relations*, 17: 135-151.

Mandel, Robert (2001). The Privatization of Security, *Armed Forces & Society*, 28: 129-151.

Mansfield, Duncan (2005). Migrant Patrols Take Root Nationally, *Arizona Daily Star*, 18 July 2005. (http://www.azstarnet.com/sn/related/84560; last visited on 10 August 2008).

Marx, Gary and Dane Archer (1976). Community Police Patrols and Vigilantism, in: Jon H. Rosenbaum and Peter C. Sederberg (eds). *Vigilante Politics*, Philadelphia: University of Pennsylvania Press: 129-158.

McGirk, Jan (2000). Blood And Bullets Along the Border As Arizona's Private Posses Hunt Mexican Migrants For Sport, *Independent UK*, 6 May 2000. (http://www.commondreams.org/headlines/050600-01.htm; last visited on 15 July 2008).

Meeropol, Rachel (2006). The War on Terror Victimizes Illegal Immigrants, in: Margaret Haerens (ed). *Illegal Immigration (Opposing Viewpoints Series)*, San Diego: Greenhaven Press: 90-96.

Moses, Norton H. (1997). *Lynching and Vigilantism in the United States: An Annotated Bibliography*, Westport: Greenwood Press.

Moser, Bob (2006). Civilian Patrols Endanger Illegal Immigrants, in: Margaret Haerens (ed). *Illegal Immigration (Opposing Viewpoints Series)*, San Diego: Greenhaven Press: 138-148.

Nelan, Bruce (1993). Not Quite So Welcome Anymore, *TIME*, 2 December 1993. (http://www.time.com/time/magazine/article/0,9171,979734,00.html; last visited on 26 September 2008).

Ngai, Mae M. (2003). The Strange Career of the Illegal Alien: Immigration Restriction and Deportation Policy in the United States, 1921-1965, *Law and History Review*, 21(1): 69-107.

Nuscheler, Franz (2004). *Internationale Migration: Flucht und Asyl*, Wiesbaden: Verlag für Sozialwissenschaften.

O'Connor, Daniel, Randy Lippert, Dale Spencer and Lisa Smylie (2008). Seeing Private Security Like a State, *Criminology and Criminal Justice*, 8(2): 203-226.

Orrenius, Pia (2001). Illegal Immigration and Enforcement along the Southwest Border. (http://www.dallasfed.org/research/border/tbe_orrenius.pdf; last visited on 16 July 2008).

Paris, Margaret L. (2002). Arrest, in: Kermit L. Hall (ed). *The Oxford Guide to American Law*, New York: Oxford University Press: 37-38.

Passel, Jeffrey (March 2004). Mexican Immigration to the US: The Latest Estimates. (http://www.migrationinformation.org/usfocus/display.cfm?ID=2 08; last visited on 14 September 2008).

Portes, Alejandro and Rubén G. Rumbaut (2006). *Immigrant America: A Portrait*, Los Angeles: University of California Press.

Pratten, David and Atreyee Sen (eds) (2008). *Global Vigilantes*, New York: Columbia University Press.

Reisler, Mark (1976). Always the Laborer, Never the Citizen: Anglo Perceptions of the Mexican Immigrant during the 1920s, *The Pacific Historical Review*, 45(2): 231-254.

Rich, Frank (2006). How Hispanics Became the New Gays, *The New York Times*, 11 June 2006. (http://select.nytimes.com/2006/06/11/opinion/11rich.html?scp=3 3&sq=immigration%20mexico%20vigilante&st=cse; last visited on 26 September 2008).

Rosas, Gilberto (2006). The Thickening Borderlands: Diffused Exceptionality and 'Immigrant' Social Struggles during the 'War on Terror,' *Cultural Dynamics*, 18: 335-349.

Rudolph, Christopher (2003). Security and the Political Economy of International Migration, *The American Political Science Review*, 97(4): 603-620.

Romero, Fernando (2008). *Hyper-Border. The Contemporary U.S. – Mexico Border and Its Future*, New York: Princeton Architectural Press.

Rosenbaum, Jon H. and Peter C. Sederberg (eds) (1976). *Vigilante Politics*, Philadelphia: University of Pennsylvania Press.

Sassen, Saskia (2000). Regulating Immigration in a Global Age: A New Policy Landscape, *Annals of the American Academy of Political and Social Science*, 570: 65-77.

Sheridan, Mary Beth (2005). Immigration Law as Anti-Terrorism Tool, *The Washington Post*, 13 June 2005. (http://www.washingtonpost.com/wp-dyn/content/article/2005/06/12/AR2005061201441.html; last visited on 05 October 2008).

Stenson, Kevin and John Lea (2007). Security, Sovereignty, and Non-State Governance 'From Below,' *Canadian Journal of Law and Society*, 22(2): 9-27.

Stillwell, Cinnamon (2006). Civilian Patrols Should be encouraged on the Border, in: Margaret Haerens (ed) *Illegal Immigration (Opposing Viewpoints Series)*, San Diego: Greenhaven Press: 130-137.

Tancredo, Tom (2006). Opposition to Illegal Immigration is Not Based on Racism, in: Margaret Haerens (ed) *Illegal Immigration (Opposing Viewpoints Series)*, San Diego: Greenhaven Press: 85-89.

Tichenor, Daniel J. (2002). *Dividing Lines: The Politics of Immigration Control in America*, Princeton: Princeton University Press.

Tichenor, Daniel J. (1994). The Politics of Immigration Reform in the United States: 1981-1990, *Polity*, 26(3): 333-362.

Tirman, John (2004). *The Maze of Fear: Security and Migration after 9/11*, New York: New Press.

Tumlin, Karen C. (2004). Suspect First: How Terrorism Policy is Reshaping Immigration Policy, *California Law Review*, 92(4): 1173-1239.

U.S. Census Bureau. (2008). Statistical Abstract of the United States: 2008. Cited as: U.S. CB. (http://usa.usembassy.de/etexts/stab2008/pop.pdf; last visited on 18 August 2008).

U.S. Census Bureau. (1940). Statistical Abstract of the United States 1940. (http://www2.census.gov/prod2/statcomp/documents/1940-02.pdf; last visited on 26 September 2008).

U.S. Customs and Border Protection Agency. (2008). Border Patrol History. Cited as: U.S. CBP-Hist. (http://www.cbp.gov/xp/cgov/border_security/border_patrol/border_patrol_ohs/history.xml; last visited on 26 September 2008).

U.S. Customs and Border Protection Agency (2008). National Border Patrol Strategy. Cited as: U.S. CBP-Strat. (http://www.customs.gov/linkhandler/cgov/border_security/border_patrol/border_patrol_ohs/national_bp_strategy.ctt/national_bp_strategy.pdf; last visited on 26 September 2008).

Unknown Author (2001). 'You are either with us or against us'. (http://archives.cnn.com/2001/US/11/06/gen.attack.on.terror/; last visited on 5 October 2008).

Unknown Author (2000). Professor Predicts 'Hispanic Homeland'. (http://www.aztlan.net/homeland.htm; last visited on 21 September 2008).

Unknown Author (2005). President Meets with President Fox and Prime Minister Martin. (http://www.whitehouse.gov/news/releases/2005/03/20050323-5.html; last visited on 21 August 2008).

U.S. General Accounting Office (1997). Illegal Immigration: Southwest Border Strategy Results Inconclusive; More Evaluation Needed. Cited as: U.S. GOA. (http://www.gao.gov/archive/1998/gg98021.pdf; last visited on 05 October 2008).

U.S. Department of State. (December 2004). The United States in 2005: Who We Are Today, *Society & Values,* 9(2) (eJournal). (http://usa.usembassy.de/etexts/soc/ijse1204.pdf; last visited on 18 August 2008).

Valverde, Mariana and Michael Mopas (2004). Insecurity and the dream of targeted governance, in: Wendy Larner and William Walters (eds). *Global Governmentality: Governing International Spaces*, London and New York: Routledge.

Waldrep, Christopher (1993). *Night Riders: Defending Community in the Black Patch*, Durham: Duke University Press.

Walker, Christopher J. (2007). Border Vigilantism and Comprehensive Immigration Reform, *Harvard Latino Law Review,* 10: 136-174.

Weiner, Myron (1995). Ethics, National Sovereignty and the Control of Immigration, *International Migration Review*, 30(1), Special Issue: Ethics, Migration, and Global Stewardship: 171-197.

Weiner, Myron (1995). *The Global Migration Crisis. Challenge to States and to Human Rights*, New York: HarperCollins College Publishers.

Wister, Owen (1998). *The Virginian*, New York: Oxford University Press.

Wood, Jennifer and Benoît Dupont (eds) (2006). *Democracy, Society and the Governance of Security*, New York: Cambridge University Press.

Yack, Bernard (2001). Popular Sovereignty and Nationalism, *Political Theory*, 29(4): 517-536.

Zinn, Howard (1999). *A People's History of the United States: 1492-Present*, New York: HarperCollins Publishers.

LEGAL DOCUMENTS
Arizona Revised Statutes (cited as: Ariz.Rev.Stat.)
http://www.azleg.gov/ArizonaRevisedStatutes.asp

Arizona Proposition 202 – Stop Illegal Hiring Initiative
http://www.azsos.gov/election/2008/Info/PubPamphlet/english/Prop202.htm; http://stopillegalhiring.com/

E-Verify
http://www.dhs.gov/xprevprot/programs/gc_1185221678150.shtm

Immigration and Nationality Act.
http://www.uscis.gov/propub/DocView/slbid/1/2

Legal Arizona Workers Act
http://www.azleg.gov/legtext/48leg/1r/bills/hb2779c.pdf

Safe Act
http://thomas.loc.gov/cgi-bin/bdquery/z?d108:s.01709:

United States Code (cited as: U.S.C.).
http://www4.law.cornell.edu/uscode/

United States Constitution (cited as U.S. Const.).
http://www.law.cornell.edu/constitution/constitution.overview.html

United States Citizenship and Immigration Services: Immigration Legislation Summary (cited as: U.S. CIS).
http://www.uscis.gov/portal/site/uscis/menuitem.eb1d4c2a3e5b9ac89243c6a7543f6d1a/?vgnextoid=dc60e1df53b2f010VgnVCM1000000ecd190aRCRD&vgnextchannel=dc60e1df53b2f010VgnVCM1000000ecd190aRCRD

COURT CASES CITED
District of Columbia v. Heller (26 June 2008)
http://www.supremecourtus.gov/opinions/07pdf/07-290.pdf

Beard v. U.S. (27 March 1895)
http://supreme.justia.com/us/158/550/case.html

WEBSITES OF ORGANIZATIONS
- Minuteman Civil Defense Corps: http://www.minutemanhq.com/ (cited as MCDC 2008)
- Minuteman Project: http://www.minutemanproject.com/
- Save Our State: http://saveourstate.org
- Desert Invasion: www.desertinvasion.us
- Declaration Alliance: http://www.declarationalliance.org/
- Friends of the Border Patrol: http://www.friendsoftheborderpatrol.com/
- American Border Patrol: http://www.americanborderpatrol.com/
- NoInvaders: http://www.noinvaders.org/home.shtml

APPENDICES

APPENDIX 1: Overview of Major U.S. Immigration Legislation

Historical Period	*Legislation/Year*	*Major Provisions*
Gilded Age	Immigration Act (1790)	First federal activity in an area previously under the control of the individual states; establishes a uniform rule for naturalization; sets residence requirement at 2 yrs.
	Aliens Act (1798)	First federal law pertinent to immigration rather than naturalization; authorizes President to arrest and/or deport any alien deemed dangerous to the U.S.
	Steerage Act (1819)	First significant Federal law relating to immigration; establishes continuing reporting of immigration to the U.S. (Secretary of State & Congress) by vessel; restricts number of passengers on all vessels coming to or leaving the U.S.
	Immigration Act (1864)	First Congressional attempt to centralize control of immigration; appoints Commissioner of Immigration
	Immigration Act (1875)	Establishes policy of direct federal regulation of immigration; bars for the first

		time entry to undesirable immigrants; bars prostitutes and criminals
	Chinese Exclusion Act (1882)	Makes Chinese laborers inadmissible
	Immigration Act (1882)	First general immigration law; establishes system of central control of immigration; adds to classes of undesirables: convicts, „lunatics," „idiots," and those „likely to become a public charge;" establishes head tax on immigrants
	Contract Labor Act (1885)	Prohibits contract labor admissions
	Chinese Exclusion Act (1888)	Extends Chinese exclusion
	Immigration Act (1891)	First comprehensive law for national control of immigration; creates federal immigration bureaucracy; authorizes deportation of illegal aliens; adds to classes of undesirables: "persons suffering from certain contagious disease," criminals, "polygamists," "aliens assisted by others by payment of passage;" forbids encouragement of immigration by means of advertisement
Progressive Era and 1920s	**Immigration Act (1903)**	First measure to provide for exclusion of aliens on the

	grounds of proscribed opinion; adds "anarchists" to list of undesirables; extends deportation
Immigration Act (1907) ("Gentlemen's Agreement")	Creates Dillingham Commission; increases head tax; creates new exclusion categories: "imbeciles," "feeble-minded," "persons with physical and mental defects," "persons afflicted with tuberculosis," children without parents, persons who committed crimes involving moral turpitude, and prostitutes; severely limits Japanese immigration
Immigration Act (1917)	Imposes literacy test for admission; excludes all illiterates; bars virtually all Asians from entry
National Quota Law (1921)	Limits immigration of each nationality to 3% of the number of foreign-born of that nationality living in the U.S. in 1910
National Origins Act (1924)	Sets annual quotas for each nationality at 2% of the numbers of persons of that nationality in the U.S. as determined by the 1890 census
Immigration Act (1924)	Establishes U.S. Border Patrol
Immigration Act	Adds two deportable classes of aliens; makes reentry of

		(1929)	previously deported alien a felony
New Deal and World War II Years	**Immigration Act (1940)**		INS transferred from Labor to Justice Department as national security measure
	Alien Registration Act (1940)		Requires registration and fingerprinting of all aliens over 14 yrs. of age; extends list of deportable classes of immigrants
	Immigration Act (1943) ("Bracero Program")		Provides for importation of temporary agricultural laborers from North, South, and Central America; serves as legal basis for Mexican "Bracero Program"
	Act of December 17 (1943)		Repeals Chinese exclusion in favor of meager quotas
The 1940s and 1950s	War Brides Act (1945)		Allows for immigration of foreign-born spouses and children of U.S. military personnel
	Displaced Persons Act (1948)		Facilitates admission of European refugees
	Agricultural Act (1949)		Facilitates entry of seasonal farm workers; extends Bracero-Program; establishes reception centers at or near Mexican border; guarantees performance by employers in transportation and wage matters; provides workers

		with free housing and adequate meals at a reasonable cost
	Internal Security Act (1950)	Intends to strengthen security screening for immigrants; expands grounds for both exclusion and deportation; establishes alien registry
	Immigration Act (1951)	Amends Agricultural Act of 1949
	Immigration and Nationality Act (1952) ("INA")	Reaffirms national origins quota system; adds new grounds for exclusion based on political activities, ideology, and sexual preference; eliminates race as a bar to immigration; introduces alien address report system; establishes central index of all aliens in the U.S. for use by security and enforcement agencies
	Refugee Relief Act (1953)	Grants permanent residence to 214,000 European refugees
	Refugee-Escapee Act (1957)	Grants special status to refugees fleeing communist regimes
The 1960s and 1970s	Cuban Refugee Act (1960)	Begins Cuban Refugee Program
	Immigration Act (1961)	Liberalizes quota provisions of the Immigration and Na-

		tionality Act of 1952
	Refugee Assistance Act (1963)	Extends cash, medical, and educational support to refugees
	Bracero Reauthorization (1964)	Terminates Bracero Program
	Immigration and Nationality Act Amendments (1965) ("Hart-Celler Act")	Dismantles national origins quotas; begins seven-category preference system with an emphasis on family reunification
	Immigration Act (1968)	Omnibus crimes control and safe streets legislation; declares it illegal for illegal aliens to receive, possess, or carry firearms
	Social Security Act Amendments (1972)	Provides that Social Security numbers be assigned to aliens at time of lawful admission
	Indochina Refugee Act (1975)	Begins Indochinese resettlement program
	Immigration and Nationality Act Amendments (1976)	Sets per country limits (20K) for both the Eastern and Western Hemispheres
	Indochinese Refugee Act (1977)	Admits 174,988 refugees from Indochina
The 1980s and 1990s	Refugee Act (1980)	Adopts UN definition of "refugee"; expands annual refugee admissions

Immigration and Nationality Act Amendments (1981)	Authorizes INS to seize vehicles without having to establish whether the owner was involved in the illegal activity in question
Immigration Reform and Control Act (1986) ("IRCA")	Grants amnesty/permanent residence to 3 million undocumented aliens; imposes watered-down employer sanctions; establishes immigrant antidiscrimination agency in Justice Dept.; initiates special agricultural worker program
Immigration Act (1990)	Increases annual immigration cap to 675,000; reaffirms family reunification preferences but adds employment-based and "diversity" visas
Immigration Act (1993) ("North American Free-Trade Agreement Implementation Act")	Facilitates temporary entry for immigrants from Canada and Mexico; establishes procedures for temporary entry
Violent Crime Control and Law Enforcement Act (1994)	Authorizes establishment of a criminal alien tracking center; revised deportation procedures; provides for improved border management; strengthens penalties for passport and visa offenses
Antiterrorism and Effective Death Pen-	Expedites procedures for removal of alien terrorists;

alty Act (1996) ("AEDPA")	establishes measures for exclusion of members of terrorist organizations; modifies procedures for identification and processing of alien terrorists; establishes criminal alien identification system
Personal Responsibility and Work Opportunity Reconciliation Act (1996)	Limits immigrant access to public welfare benefits
Illegal Immigration Reform and Individual Responsibility Act (1996) ("IIRIRA")	Strengthens border enforcement and employer sanctions; expedites the deportation process; establishes exceptions for non-citizen access to public benefits

Sources: Tichenor 2002:3-5; U.S. Citizenship and Immigration Services Website.

APPENDIX 2: Overview Immigration Legislation after September 11, 2001

Historical Period	Legislation/Year	Major Provisions
After 2001	**USA Patriot Act (2001)**	Expands the authority of U.S. law enforcement agencies for the stated purpose of fighting terrorism; enhances the discretion of law enforcement and immigration authorities in detaining and deporting immigrants suspected of terrorism-related acts
	Change of Address Requirement (2001)	Renews enforcement of Section 265(a) of the Immigration and Nationality Act of 1952; requires non-citizens to submit change-of-address forms to the government within ten days of moving residences
	Enhanced Border Security and Visa Entry Reform Act (2002)	Requires biometric data readers and scanners at all ports of entry; extends the deadline for border crossing identification cards (Laser Visas) to contain a biometric identifier that matches the biometric characteristic of the card

	holder
The Smart Border Agreement (2002)	Bilateral national security program signed both by the United States and Mexico; plan to build a "smart" border; program includes 22 points ranging from pre-screening travelers to electronic exchange of information between the two governments and their agencies
Homeland Security Act (2002)	Increases federal law enforcement agencies' citizen surveillance powers; creates Department of Homeland Security; replaces the INS
The Aviation Transportation and Security Act (2002)	Requires all airport baggage screeners to be U.S. citizens
Intelligence Reform and Terrorism Prevention Act (2004)	Adds 2000 additional Border Patrol agents at U.S.-Mexico border; requires the integration of the entry and exit data system with other databases and data systems
Proposition 200: Arizona (2004)	Requires employees of the local and state governments to verify the immigration status

	of people seeking government benefits and report any violations to federal officials; considers failure to report a criminal offense; requires proof of citizenship in order to register to vote
Intelligence Reform and Terrorism Prevention Act (2004)	Creates position of Director of National Intelligence; creates the National Counterterrorism Center; establishes National Intelligence Council; calls for increase of border patrol agents by at least 2,000 per year between 2006 and 2010; increases penalties for human smuggling; provides extraterritorial federal jurisdiction over offenses related to weapons of mass destruction
Real ID Act (2005)	Orders security studies to be done at the border; authorizes DHS Secretary to "all laws as necessary" to expedite the construction of barriers and roads along the border

Border Protection, Antiterrorism, and Illegal Immigration Control Act ("Sensenbrenner Bill") (2005) (not enacted)	Bill passed by the House but not passed by the Senate; would have authorized 700 miles of new walls and fences along the border, extended the definition of "smuggling", made "unlawful presence" a felony and called for local law officers involvement in immigration enforcement
Secure Fence Act (2006)	Involves the construction of a 700-mile fence along the border

Sources: Tichenor 2002: 3-5; see also Romero 2008; Reimers 1998.

Hamburger Studien zur Kriminologie und Kriminalpolitik
hrsg. von Prof. Dr. Susanne Krasmann, Prof. Dr. Fritz Sack, Prof. Dr. Sebastian Scheerer, Prof. Dr. Klaus Sessar, Prof. Dr. Bernhard Villmow und Prof. Dr. Peter Wetzels

Thorsten Kruwinnus
Das enge und das weite Verständnis der Kriminalsoziologie bei Franz Exner
Eine vergleichend-werkimmanente Vorstudie
Erst jüngst hat Walter Fuchs die Verstrickung des kontroversen Kriminologen Franz Exner in die NS-Kriminalpolitik am Beispiel von dessen Mitarbeit am NS-Gemeinschaftsfremdengesetz analysiert. Nunmehr beleuchtet Thorsten Kruwinnus sozusagen das andere Gesicht des Franz Exner: das des überragenden Förderers einer Kriminalsoziologie in der Weimarer Republik, der als guter Schüler Franz v. Liszts seine Hoffnung auf wissenschaftliche Aufklärung gesetzt hatte und in manchen Dingen seiner Zeit voraus war. Ein kurzer, knapper und inspirierender Beitrag zu einem wichtigen Aspekt der Kriminologiegeschichte des 20. Jahrhunderts. Prof. Dr. Sebastian Scheerer
Bd. 45, 2009, 128 S., 19,90 €, br., ISBN 978-3-643-10162-4

LIT Verlag Berlin – Münster – Wien – Zürich – London
Auslieferung Deutschland / Österreich / Schweiz: siehe Impressumsseite

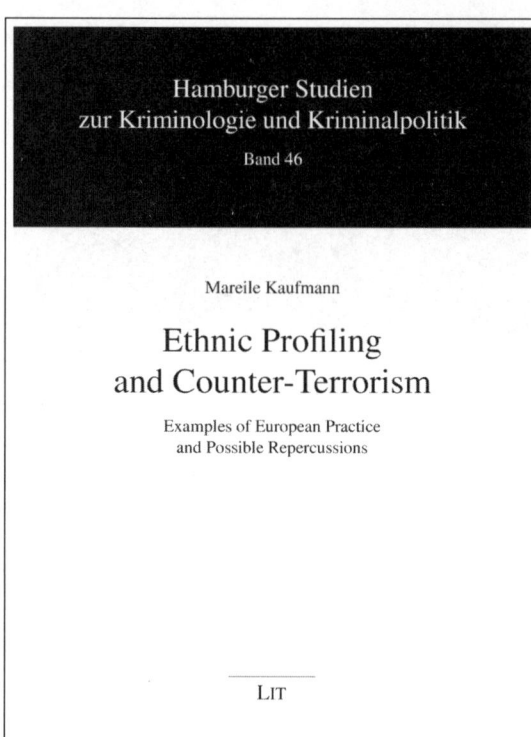

Mareile Kaufmann
Ethnic Profiling and Counter-Terrorism
Examples of European Practice and Possible Repercussions
This work introduces examples of ethnic profiling in European counter-terrorism and analyzes possible after-effects on a theoretical basis. Primary effects, which are generally considered positive, are contrasted with secondary effects and methodological breaches, for instance the over- and under-inclusion of a profile, substitution and negative effects on the social life of the targeted group. The implications are documented with examples taken from the European counter-terrorism context and discussed in relation to European legal standards. The discussion closes with a proportionality test.
Bd. 46, 2010, 128 S., 19,90 €, br., ISBN 978-3-643-10447-2